Staying Well

Staying Well

Highlighting Hazards, Highlighting Health

for

Missionaries in Japan

Janet Dallman

Copyright © 2021 Janet Dallman
All rights reserved.
ISBN-13: 9798517415547

Quotes used with permission:

Bloecher, Detlef. (2005) 'Reducing Missionary Attrition (ReMAP) - what it said and what it did', p.11. Used with permission.

Bloecher, Detlef. (No date) 'Good agency practices – lessons from ReMAP II', p.8. Used with permission.

Bloecher, Detlef. (2004) 'Good Agency Practices: Lessons from ReMAP II'. Connections: The Journal of the WEA Missions Commission, 3 (2), p.12. Used with permission.

Bosch, Brenda. (2014) *Thriving in Difficult Places*, Volume 1 p. 7, 59, 153, 273; Volume 3 p. 153. www.thrivingmember.com Used with permission.

Brown, Ronald. 'Preparing for the Realities of Missions in a Changing World', (Evangelical Missions Quarterly October- December 2006, Volume 42, Issue 4). Used with permission.

Carmichael, Amy. Compiled by Bee Trehane. *Fragments that Remain* (Fort Washington, PA: CLC Publications,1987, e-book 2013). Used with permission.

David, R. (2019) 'Editorial: Elder Member Care', Global Member Care Network (GMCN). Used with permission.

Doughill, John. (2016) *In Search of Japan's Hidden Christians*, p.17, 24. UK: SPCK Reproduced with permission of the Licensor through PLSclear.

Fujiwara, Atsuyoshi. (2012) *Theology of Culture in a Japanese Context*, p.228, 276. Oregon: Pickwick Publications. Used by permission of Wipf and Stock Publishers, www.wipfandstock.com

Gardner, Laura Mae. (2015) *Healthy Resilient, and Effective in Cross-Cultural Ministry – A Comprehensive Member Care Plan*, p.15. Indonesia: Katalis Gloria. Used with permission.

Gosden, Eric. (1982). *The Other Ninety-Nine*, p.20, 79. (London: Marshalls Paperbacks & The Japan Evangelistic Band). Used with permission.

Intervarsity. 'What Spiritual Warfare Is (and What It Definitely Isn't)'. Accessed on 27th May 2020 at: https://intervarsity.org/blog/what-spiritual-warfare-and-what-it-definitely-isn't Used with permission.

Lee, Samuel C. (2011) *Understanding Japan: Through the eyes of Christian faith*, p.90, 145. Fourth Edition. Amsterdam: Foundation University Press. Used with permission.

Schaefer, Frauke. C & Schaefer, Charles. A. (2012) *Trauma & Resilience: A Handbook*, p.93 Used with permission.

Selvey, David. (October 24, 2015) 'The Truth of Missionary Attrition' at: The Truth of Missionary Attrition – Faith Blogs (faithlafayette.org). Used with permission.

Van Ochs, B. 'Ten Challenges That May Make Going Home Look Attractive', (Evangelical Missions Quarterly October-December 2001, Volume 37, Issue 4). Used with permission.

Scripture quotations marked (NIV) are taken from the Holy Bible, New International Version®, NIV®. Copyright © 1973, 1978, 1984, 2011 by Biblica, Inc.® Used by permission of Zondervan. All rights reserved worldwide. www.zondervan.com The "NIV" and "New International Version" are trademarks registered in the United States Patent and Trademark Office by Biblica, Inc.®

Cover photo by Devin H on Unsplash

Contents

Foreword ix
Preface xiii
How to read this book xv
Introduction xvii
Chapter 1: Highlighting Hazards 1
Highlighting Hazards: Workbook 13
Chapter 2: Highlighting Health 19
Highlighting Health: Workbook 37
Chapter 3: Recommendations & Reflections for Self-care & Agency Member Care ... 45
Conclusion 63
Appendix A1: Japan Member Care Survey - Missionary Questionnaire 65
Appendix A2: Individual Missionaries Survey – Demographic Data 75
Appendix A3: What factors led missionaries to leave Japan? 79
Appendix A4: What enables missionaries to stay in Japan? 81
Appendix B1: Semi-structured interview questions 83
Appendix B2: Interviewee data 85
Appendix C: Research methodology 87
Appendix D: Japanese context 93
Glossary 103
Bibliography 111
About the Author 125

Foreword

It was in the trenches of Japanese language school where I first got to know Janet Dallman and her husband Peter. Coming to Japan from two different cultures, me from America and the Dallmans from the UK, we enjoyed learning from each other's worldviews, strengths, and weaknesses. We also soon came to learn that our greatest common bond was our calling and passion to spread the good news of the life-transforming gospel with those who are eager for hope. Our life's desire was to share the living water in the spiritually parched desert of Japan.

Even though we served with different mission agencies, our common desire to share the gospel message has given us opportunities to work together on a number of occasions. For the past several years, I have had the privilege of serving as President of the Japan Evangelical Missionary Association (JEMA; jema.org), a network of Protestant mission agencies and missionaries that has over 1,000 members who are focused on reaching the Japanese. Janet and Peter have served the mission community in various roles over the years. Most recently, they have been in leadership roles in JEMA's Member Care Ministry, providing member care and training member care givers.

Staying Well is largely a product of Janet's extensive research in the missionary community across many different fronts. It has been reviewed, processed, and field tested with the leaders of mission agencies in Japan at our annual JEMA convention, where it received high praise. An overwhelming desire was expressed to see this put into book form to serve the mission community in Japan.

I know from personal experience how essential member care is and must be in today's climate of cross-cultural ministry. It's vital for those who desire to run hard and finish well. Her many years of service in Japan, which has been dubbed the missionary graveyard, and her academic studies in missionary member care make Janet extremely qualified to speak into this area from so many angles.

Staying Well is an excellent resource to add to your personal ministry library as well as to encourage your fellow workers. I envisage it becoming a go-to resource for help in maintaining the delicate balance of a healthy, striving ministry. While it is written with the specific viewpoint of maintaining missionary health in Japan, I believe these same principles can easily be contextualized to any cross-cultural ministry situation. I highly recommend *Staying Well* as a must-read book for anyone in cross-cultural ministry, especially those who are just getting started.

As a cool drink of water refreshes the soul, *Staying Well* is a great resource to maintain refreshment in ministry as we share the Living Water to those who thirst.

Nathan Snow, President
Japan Evangelical Missionary Association (JEMA)

After having served in Japan for about seven years, my family spent a month in the fall of 1989 at a residential facility in California that assists missionaries and pastors struggling with ministry-related issues. Things weren't going at all well for us physically, emotionally, or spiritually, and we needed the type of counselling and spiritual input that would put us on a better path for life and ministry. After that helpful time at the residential facility, we made the difficult decision to leave Japan and transition to pastoral ministry in the US.

Since 2012, my wife and I have served with Barnabas International, shepherding and encouraging the hearts of global servants around the world. Our deepest desire is to see missionaries live in healthy ways as they fulfil their God-given calling.

I first met Janet Dallman in Japan and experienced a real kinship with her and her heart for member care. And as leaders of the Member Care Ministry of the Japan Evangelical Missionary Association (JEMA), we have been so grateful for Janet's faithful service on the committee. I have come to know Janet as a student of God's Word and as someone deeply invested in finding ways to enhance the member care of OMF, the organization under whom she serves. Therefore, it didn't come as a surprise to me that her Master's degree resulted in this book. I was present when Janet shared her findings at the JEMA Connect meeting in February 2020, which provided the participants much helpful and practical information.

In our ever-changing world, and especially during the past year of the pandemic, missionaries have had to endure many significant challenges, both personal and ministry related. These challenges have taken their toll on the physical, emotional, relational, and spiritual lives of those who have sought to share Jesus with those who have not heard his name. In the midst of these challenges, it is often difficult to grasp how best to stay well—how to thrive in Japan as a missionary.

Staying Well has come at just the right time. Janet has put together a well-researched, well-thought-through resource that will greatly benefit missionaries and the organizations that want to provide well for their members. This is not a book about theory, but rather one that speaks to the practical needs of missionaries and how they can stay well in their lives and service. The worksheets alone are well worth the cost of the book.

As I look back on my own missionary experience in the 1980s, I can see that my life may have turned out differently had I had access to the material Janet has shared in this book. Would it have made a difference? Only God knows. But I do know that it will make a difference in the life of any missionary who reads it.

My prayer is that God will use *Staying Well* in the lives of many missionaries and their organizations to enhance the work of the gospel in Japan and beyond.

Alan Steier
Barnabas International

Preface

This book is mainly for missionaries to Japan—both current and future—and their mission agencies. I hope it will also be of interest to churches that send and support missionaries and others who train and encourage missionaries in their fields of service.

During my 23 years of missionary service in Japan, I've rejoiced in welcoming many missionaries to Japan, but I've also been saddened as many others have left. Although many left Japan for good reasons, I can't help but wonder if some might have stayed longer if they'd had access to better care or if they had taken advantage of care that was available to them. Keeping missionaries on the field is even more critical since fewer new missionaries are coming to Japan. Missionary numbers have dropped from 2,800 in the mid-1980s to just 1,700 in 2016. That's a massive drop of almost 40% in 30 years,[1] although missionary numbers have improved somewhat in the last five years.

Added to all this, the Japanese are the world's second largest unevangelised people group (in terms of the number of people who haven't been exposed to the gospel) and the Christian population is less than 1%.[2] Therefore, fewer new missionaries and the possible premature exit of trained and experienced missionaries are major concerns for the evangelisation of Japan.

Driven by a desire to see missionaries thrive and Japanese people come to know Christ — still too great a task for the Japanese church to achieve alone — I studied missionary attrition and retention in Japan for my Master's degree (2019). In other words, I investigated what causes missionaries to leave and what keeps them going in tough times. I wanted to consider how to enable flourishing, long term missionary service, benefitting both missionaries and God's Kingdom in Japan. This book shares my discoveries. It also offers practical suggestions for self-care and care by mission agencies for missionaries in Japan.

The Introduction sets the context for the rest of the book. It includes my personal story, information about the Japanese Christian and missionary context and general information about missionary attrition and retention. (Because this book is written to be accessible and immediately applicable to missionaries and agencies in Japan, I haven't written extensively about these subjects, but my sources are given in the bibliography.)

The rest of the book is divided into three chapters and a conclusion. The first one, Highlighting Hazards, looks at why missionaries left Japan, while the second one, Highlighting Health, considers what helps missionaries thrive in Japan. The worksheets at the end of both chapters are designed to help missionaries and mission agencies put self-care and organisational care practices in place. Finally, the third chapter offers reflections and recommendations for self-care and mission agency care for missionaries to Japan.

The main text includes some statistics and graphs from the survey (218 participants) and interviews (15 people, selected from the survey respondents), while Appendix A2 contains survey participants' demographic data and Appendix B2 gives interviewee information. Appendix C gives details of the methods used for the survey and interviews, and Appendix D provides an overview of the Japanese context and how this affects missionaries to Japan.

I hope and pray that this book will help missionaries in Japan to stay well in their service, as they seek to extend God's kingdom.

Finally, I'm thankful to: missionaries to Japan, for serving God amongst the Japanese people and for their cooperation with my research project; OMF, for encouraging and enabling me to pursue my studies; the tutors of Redcliffe College, for their patient encouragement and practical help; the Japan Evangelical Missionary Association (JEMA), for the opportunity to share this material with the missionary community in Japan; Simon Pleasants, Bea Neblung and Wendy Marshall, for giving their time to edit this book.

Above all, I'm thankful to my husband, Peter, for his unwavering support and to God for His help — not only in completing my Master's degree and writing this book, but for saving me and sustaining me in service in Japan thus far, despite the many, many times I too have wanted to leave.

---

[1] Mehn, John Wm. (2017) *Multiplying Churches in Japanese Soil*, p.4. Pasadena: William Carey Library

[2] Joshua Project (2019) 'Unreached Listings: 100 Largest Unreached Peoples'. Frontier Ventures. Accessed on 1st April 2019 at:
https://joshuaproject.net/unreached/1?limit=100&s%5B0%5D=WorkersNeeded&o=desc

How to read this book

This book is divided into three main chapters.

Chapter one, Highlighting Hazards, looks at the reasons why missionaries left Japan. If you want to consider potential pitfalls or challenges that may lie ahead, start reading here!

Chapter two, Highlighting Health, considers what helps missionaries to thrive in Japan. Begin here if you already know the pitfalls or want to begin with the more positive aspects of how to thrive in Japan.

Chapter three offers reflections and recommendations for self-care and mission-agency care for missionaries to Japan. If you want to skip the data and jump straight to my conclusions, this is where to begin.

At the end of the first two chapters, I have included worksheets to help you convert what you have read into practical ways forward for self-care and organisational care. Some worksheets are for individual use, while others can be done in groups or with your mission agency. I recommend that you pray as you begin and keep a journal on hand to note things that stand out for you, how God is speaking to you, and what practical steps you will take as a result. You don't have to do the worksheets, but if you want to apply the lessons from this book to your own life, ministry and mission agency, I highly recommend them.

If you're the sort of person who loves statistics, detail and wants to know the whys and wherefores, ins and outs of my research, check out the appendices! They explain the basis for my research, the methods I used, and the Japanese context, as well as provide statistics and graphs that didn't easily 'fit' into the main part of the book.

Ultimately, you decide how to read this book! You can read it in the order it is written or read the sections that appeal to you or which you feel most in need of right now. In whatever way you read this book, I pray that God will use it to speak to you, highlighting hazards you might be facing, providing tips on how to avoid them, and helping you put self-care practices in place — all for His Kingdom in Japan!

Introduction

I have welcomed many missionaries to Japan, but I've also seen an awful lot of them leave. Why? Here are some real examples.

One family left because of physical and mental health challenges. A single missionary left because her vision and her organisation's didn't 'fit'. Several missionaries left to care for elderly parents. Yet others left because of their children's education or adult children's need for support. Some left because their church called them back. Some left because of struggles with Japanese language and culture. I could go on.

Now, let me just say upfront that I don't believe that it is always right to stay in Japan, but could any of these godly, committed missionaries have been prevented from leaving? Moreover, how can those who remain in Japan thrive in ministry, rather than "limp along at...reduced efficiency..."[1]?

From a human perspective, whenever missionaries leave Japan earlier than expected, they and their colleagues may feel a sense of disappointment, waste and dashed hopes of anticipated fruitful ministry. All the ploughing and sowing — the Bible training, the prayer and financial support, the effort poured into language and culture learning, and the relationships formed in Japan — and for what harvest?

Make no mistake, the cost of missionary attrition is huge. One author has commented, "The statistics are serious, the financial implications...dramatic and calculable, but the human and emotional implications are staggering and incalculable."[2] Another poignantly adds, 'lost souls are not reached, churches go unplanted, "windows of opportunity are lost"'.[3]

I write this book as someone who is no stranger to struggling with whether to stay in Japan or return home. Over 23 years with OMF International in Japan, my husband Peter and I have wrestled with this on several occasions. During my initial months as a frustrated, culture-shocked language learner, I lost count of the number of times I told Peter, "I don't know what you're doing, but I'm leaving!"[4] I stayed, but it was touch-and-go for a while! A few years later, Peter developed depression, and we left Japan for two and a half years with no assurance of return. Further down the line, we struggled to stay in Japan due to leadership and management issues. Recent years have seen us struggle with physical health, role-related questions and concern for elderly parents.

How long should we stay in Japan and what does it mean to stay well? We have struggled and continue to struggle with these questions.

However, this struggle shouldn't come as a surprise. The devil isn't happy when missionaries share the saving news of Jesus with the Japanese and he "prowls around like a roaring lion looking for someone to devour" (1 Peter 5:8).

Also, Japan has a reputation of being a hard place to serve as a missionary. It has sometimes been called a missionary graveyard[5]. And with good reason.

Japan's Christian history began fruitfully, but was followed by cycles of intense persecution and martyrdom. Christians in Japan today represent less than 1% of the population, many churches are slow-growing, and numerous places lack adequate Christian witness.

Thankfully, Japanese Christians and missionaries no longer face the threat of persecution or death. However, many Japanese Christians experience prejudice, and missionaries continue to face the challenges of learning the Japanese language and culture, the wariness of Japanese towards organized religion, and the cultural pressures that make it hard for Japanese people to embrace Jesus.

This disheartening situation and enormous task can cause missionaries to feel overwhelmed and discouraged. Indeed, Japan is a hard place to be a missionary. In his novel *Silence*, Japanese Christian author Shusaku Endo uses the picture of a swamp to describe the ground of Japan[6]. But perhaps Japan provides another image of gospel 'soil' (Matthew 13:1-23); the farmer sows the seed, but his enemy sprays the crop with weed killer and digs it up! (Appendix D gives more details on Japan's Christian and mission history.)

Japan's reputation for being a hard place to serve is reflected in the statistics of how long missionaries serve in the country. The chart (below) shows the length of active missionary service in Japan.

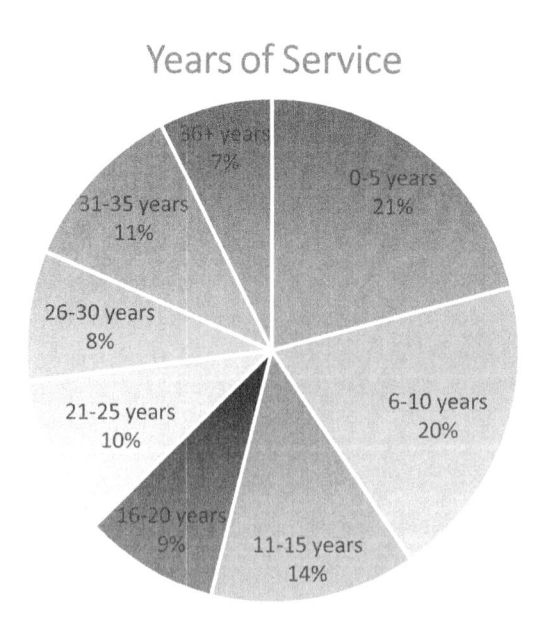

Years of Service

- 0-5 years: 21%
- 6-10 years: 20%
- 11-15 years: 14%
- 16-20 years: 9%
- 21-25 years: 10%
- 26-30 years: 8%
- 31-35 years: 11%
- 36+ years: 7%

Significantly, more than 40% of missionaries left after spending a decade or less in Japan.

On average, missionaries to Japan take nearly eight years to adjust[7], meaning many leave *before* they adjust. Add to this that it takes the average (native English speaking) missionary more than two years to learn Japanese (from zero) and that personal experience shows that ministry competence takes upwards of seven years. So this figure is concerning.

Therefore, it is vital that missionaries and mission agencies do all they can to prevent premature attrition and examine positive retention factors in order to promote thriving, effective service amongst missionaries in Japan for the extension of God's Kingdom.

The vision

The vision behind this book has been with me a long time. Even before becoming a missionary to Japan, I longed to care for missionaries pastorally and spiritually. My mission upbringing and experience exposed me to some of the struggles that make up the lives of missionaries, and I longed to help. This book arises out of my long-held desire to encourage and care for missionaries, and out of my own experience of struggling to stay and 'stay well' in Japan.

This desire led me to take a Master's degree in member care for missionaries. For my research project, I chose to examine factors that cause missionaries to leave Japan (attrition) and factors that help them to stay (retention), along with ways agencies can facilitate flourishing, long-term service. The subsequent chapters are based on the results of this research.

My hope is that this book will function in a similar way to the Japanese health check-up — providing preventative rather than reactive care. Of course, both types of care are important, but with a little more preventative care, we might be able to avoid the need for some reactive care. A simple example of preventative care would be maintaining a healthy pattern of regular days off and vacation or holiday time. Over the long term, such patterns of life should lead to greater physical and emotional health, thereby hopefully reducing the need for reactive care due to stress, or mental or physical ill-health.

This book seeks to help missionaries and mission agencies to highlight potential hazards in life and ministry and how to avoid them. Furthermore, it aims to highlight healthy practices of self-care and member care policies, thereby enabling missionaries to 'stay well' in Japan. My prayer is that this preventative health check-up will lead to flourishing, long-term missionary service and the increased evangelisation of Japan.

[1] Shepherd, David. L. (2014) *Promoting Missionary Mutual Care Through Spiritual Community* p.33-34. (Quoting Loss, Myron. *Culture Shock: Dealing with Stress in Cross-Cultural Living*, 1983.) Accessed on 7th May 2018 at: http://digitalcommons.georgefox.edu/cgi/viewcontent.cgi?article=1085&context=dmin

[2] Taylor, William D. (2002) 'Revisiting a Provocative Theme: The Attrition of Longer-Term Missionaries', *Missiology* 30 Issue 1, p.71. Accessed on 13th June 2018 at: http://journals.sagepub.com/doi/pdf/10.1177/009182960203000105

[3] Steffen, Tom & McKinney Davis, Lois. (2008) *Encountering Missionary Life and Work*, p.331. Grand Rapids Michigan: Baker Academic. Citing Graham's (1987) 'The cost of attrition' chart.

[4] Dallman, Janet. (2016) *Out on a Limb*, p, 44.

[5] Rayl, B & Oh, M. (2014) 'Signs of Spiritual Awakening in Japan' Accessed on 21st October 2020 at: https://www.thegospelcoalition.org/article/signs-spiritual-awakening-japan/

[6] Endo, Shusaku. (Translated by William Johnston) (1969) *Silence*. USA: Picador Modern Classics (2016)

[7] Takamoto, Susan Plumb. (2003) *Liminality and the North American missionary adjustment process in Japan*, p.127. Fuller Theological Seminary, PhD thesis. Received directly from the author.

Chapter 1: Highlighting Hazards

This chapter highlights some of the hazards faced by Christian workers in Japan by examining the reasons why missionaries left Japan. It gives a broad overview of the results of the survey and interviews I conducted for my Master's thesis, while chapter 3 provides more-detailed reflection and recommendations. (I want to stress that my aim is not to criticise individual missionaries or mission agencies, or to judge missionaries who have left Japan.)

Survey and interview results and comments

Survey results

The online survey about why missionaries left Japan was divided into five areas: personal factors, family-related factors, ministry-related factors, and mission-agency-related factors. Below, I consider each of these areas and compare them with the results for the whole survey.

(Participants scored each factor on a scale of zero (unimportant) to five (most important). Appendix A2 gives information about survey participants, Appendix A3 gives overall factors which led missionaries to leave Japan and Appendix A4 gives overall factors which help missionaries stay in Japan.)

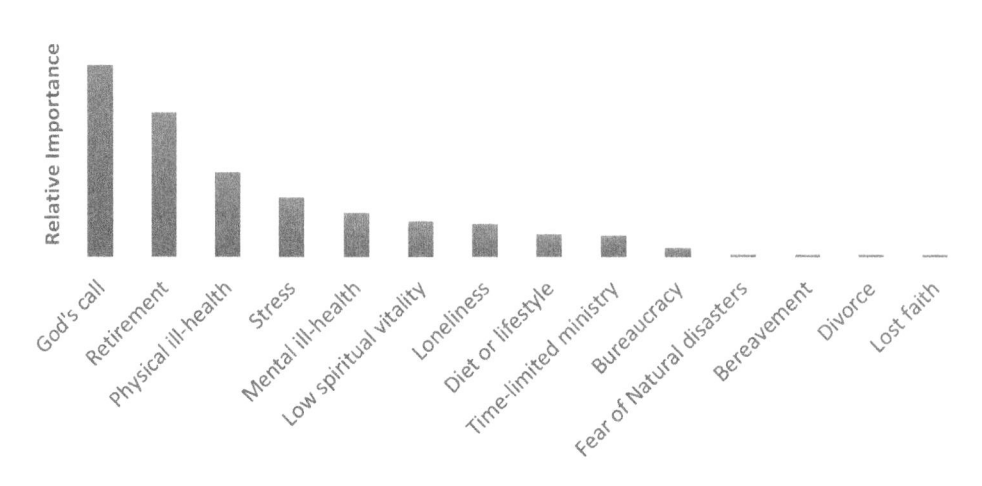

Personal factors

Personal Factors involved in Missionaries Leaving Japan

Bar chart (Relative Importance), bars from tallest to shortest: God's call, Retirement, Physical ill-health, Stress, Mental ill-health, Low spiritual vitality, Loneliness, Diet or lifestyle, Time-limited ministry, Bureaucracy, Fear of Natural disasters, Bereavement, Divorce, Lost faith.

This graph depicts the relative importance of personal reasons for why missionaries left Japan.

Encouragingly, God's call to leave Japan ranked highest (both in this category and in the whole survey). One person commented, "We felt God called us away from Japan — he released us to leave." Previous surveys on why missionaries leave their fields of service included "a lack of call" and "a change in job" amongst contributing factors, but they didn't mention a positive call to go elsewhere.[1] The current survey redresses that imbalance.

In common with previous surveys of missionaries serving in many countries[2], the next most popular answer was retirement, which isn't surprising considering the average age of those who completed the survey, roughly 51–53 years old (see Appendix A2). Retiring missionaries need support in making this transition, but apart from that it is not a cause for concern. Poor physical health ranked third, followed by stress and mental health (at similar levels). Encouragingly, most survey respondents hadn't been greatly affected by fear of natural disasters (an ever-present threat in Japan), bereavement, divorce, or loss of faith.

However, amongst those aged 30–60 years (i.e., those who left Japan before retirement age), although God's call to leave remained the highest ranked factor, stress ranked second, with mental ill-health and a low spiritual vitality joint third. This is a significant concern and has implications for mission agencies and seminaries in how they might coach missionaries in healthy living, coping with stress and in developing ongoing spiritual vitality.

Family-related factors

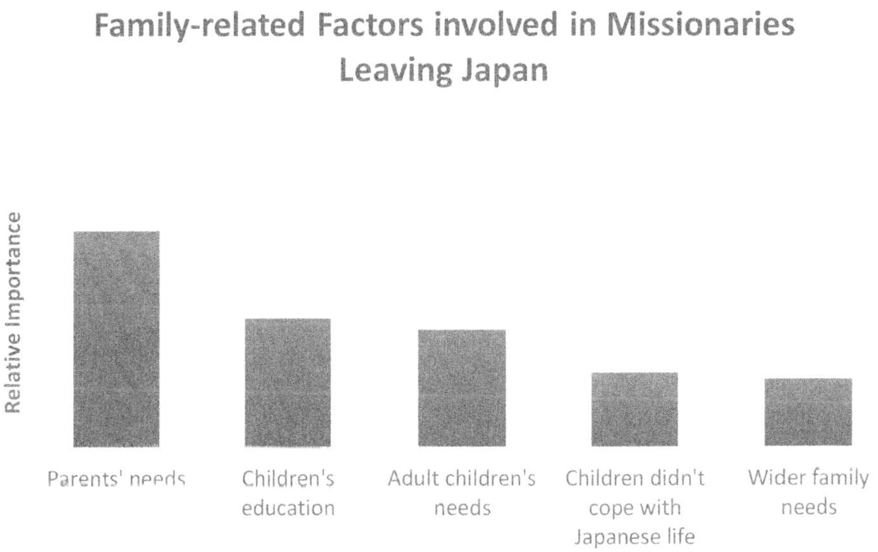

Family-related Factors involved in Missionaries Leaving Japan
Relative Importance
Parents' needs
Children's education
Adult children's needs
Children didn't cope with Japanese life
Wider family needs

Many in the missionary community are keenly aware of the difficulties in ensuring missionaries' children receive appropriate education and of how education-related issues can be a factor in missionaries' leaving Japan. However, these results show that the top family-related reason for leaving is the needs of missionaries' parents. Indeed, the needs of missionaries' parents were ranked third over all categories, compared to 15th in other surveys amongst missionaries worldwide.[3] This highlights the need to think creatively about this issue.

Nevertheless, in this category, children's concerns as a whole (children's education, children's lack of coping, and the needs of adult children) contributed most to why respondents left Japan. However, one person pointed out that "some who left for…children's education was not because provision was inadequate but…personal choice." Personally, I was surprised at how often the needs of adult children contributed to survey respondents leaving Japan.

Ministry-related factors

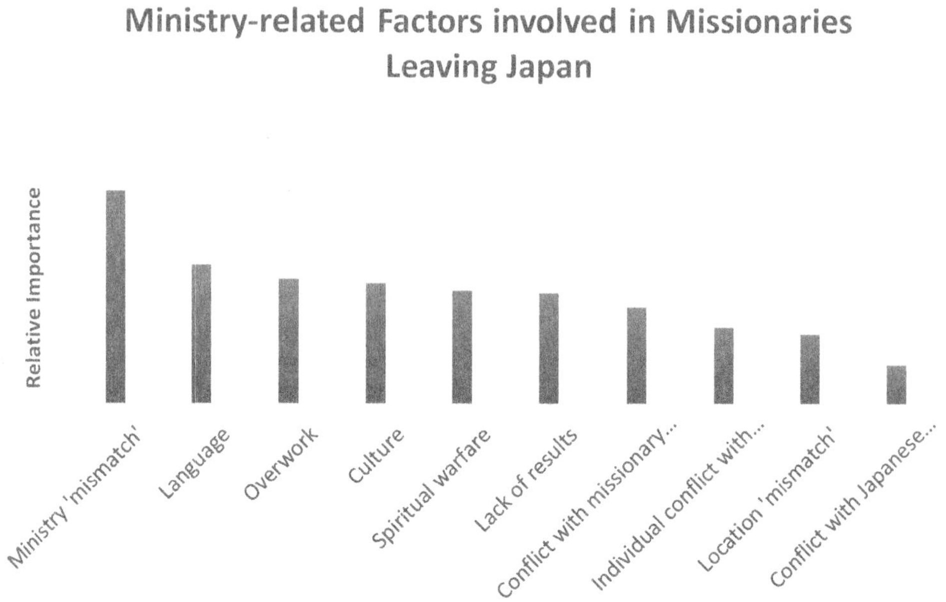
Ministry-related Factors involved in Missionaries Leaving Japan
Relative Importance
Ministry 'mismatch'
Language
Overwork
Culture
Spiritual warfare
Lack of results
Conflict with missionary...
Individual conflict with...
Location 'mismatch'
Conflict with Japanese...

Significantly, ministry mismatch ranked first in this category (fifth amongst all categories). This implies unfulfilled expectations and disillusionment, causing missionaries to leave Japan. It raises questions like how much prior knowledge do future missionaries have, or need, about where they will live, and what ministry looks like? And are agencies being careful enough in assessing and placing candidates?

The high rank of language emphasises the difficulty of learning Japanese. Many Japanese do not speak other languages well (moreover, effective ministry largely occurs in one's heart language). Overall, language ranked seventh in reasons for leaving Japan. This contrasts strikingly with other worldwide missionary surveys where "language problems" were ranked 24th amongst reasons to leave.[4] This has substantial implications for individuals and mission agencies alike. Furthermore, linguistic understanding is inextricably linked with cultural understanding (ranked fourth), and competence in both is needed, which may serve to reduce conflict with Japanese team members (ranked tenth).

Overwork is endemic in Japan. Respondents recognised its destructive consequences in their lives. This, in conjunction, with respondents' high ranking of "holiday/vacation" in factors that helped them stay in Japan (see Chapter 2), should give missionaries and mission agencies pause for thought.

Spiritual warfare in Japan is significant (see Appendix D). One respondent commented that we cannot measure the influence of spiritual attack. Certainly, I have found the spiritual battle fiercer than I expected in Japan. Amy Carmichael (a missionary first to Japan and then India) commented about Japan, "Satan is tenfold more of a reality to me today than he was in England."[5]

Rated just slightly lower than spiritual warfare was disillusionment or a lack of results. Previous surveys among missionaries worldwide have found that, unsurprisingly, job satisfaction is linked with retention.[6] Therefore, Japan's spiritual resistance and the general slowness of Japanese people to respond to the gospel need to be communicated to missionary candidates to inform their expectations of ministry in Japan. Many missionaries come to Japan expecting to be the one who makes the difference — myself included! Indeed, by his grace, God uses weak people. But somehow, without denying God's overruling and gracious work, missionaries and mission leaders need to communicate this struggle to future missionaries, or else they may become disillusioned and leave prematurely.

Agency-related factors

Agency-related Factors involved in Missionaries Leaving Japan

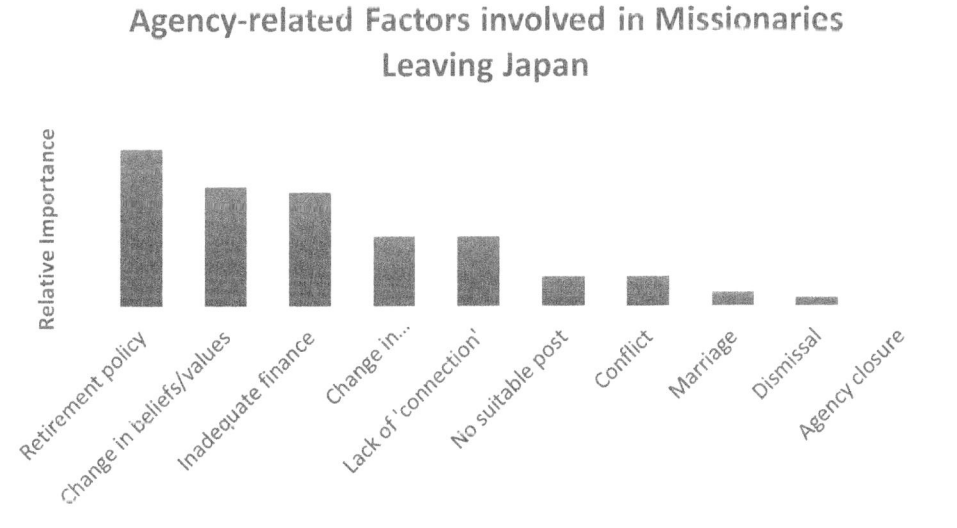

Bar chart showing relative importance of factors, in descending order: Retirement policy, Change in beliefs/values, Inadequate finance, Change in..., Lack of 'connection', No suitable post, Conflict, Marriage, Dismissal, Agency closure.

Retirement ranks top, but because this is an expected, usually healthy, reason for leaving Japan — whether through personal decision or agency policy — I will not address it here.

However, "Change in beliefs and values" is more of a concern. Even more worrying, amongst survey respondents under 60 only, "Change in beliefs or values" and "Change in vision or mission" were ranked as the top two agency-related reasons for leaving. Therefore, mission agencies' distinct characteristics are critical and must be communicated clearly to candidates and current missionaries. Furthermore, ranked the same as a "Change in vision or mission" was a feeling of a lack of connection with the agency. Agencies clearly need to consider how to nurture this, perhaps rather intangible, sense of 'connection'.

The high ranking of "Inadequate finance" will come as no surprise to many. Japan's high cost of living is demanding for long-term mission. This is true for all missionaries to Japan, but it becomes even more of an issue if family size increases and/or costly international schools are necessary or desirable. This area must be addressed practically and pastorally.

Other comments made in this section concerned leadership, either in helping missionaries stay, or in contributing to their departure. This subject also came up during the interviews and will be considered in more detail in Chapter 3 in the reflections and recommendations.

Overall survey results

To sum up, it is important to note that, except for retirement, serious illness or a strong call elsewhere, in most cases a combination of factors is involved in missionaries' decisions to leave their field of service. The top ten-ranked reasons given in the overall survey for why missionaries said they left Japan are:
(Appendix A3 gives the full results.)

Factors involved in Missionaries Leaving Japan
- Overall Survey Results

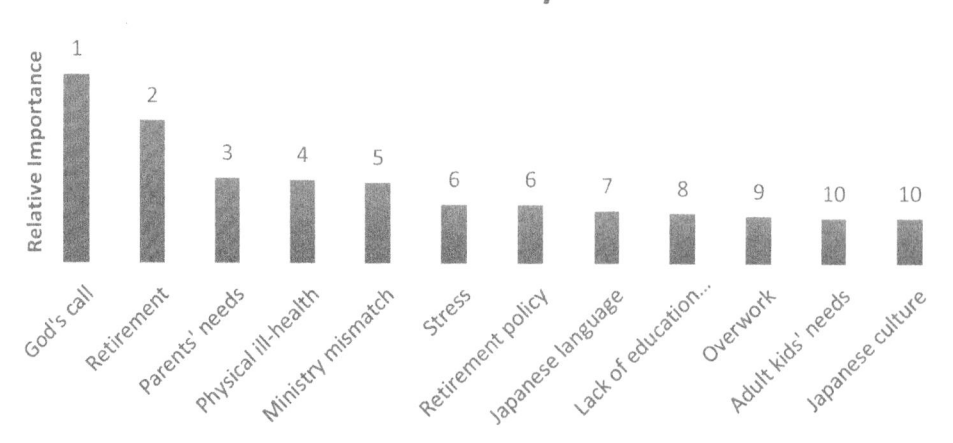

Rank	Factor
1	God's call
2	Retirement
3	Parents' needs
4	Physical ill-health
5	Ministry mismatch
6	Stress
6	Retirement policy
7	Japanese language
8	Lack of education...
9	Overwork
10	Adult kids' needs
10	Japanese culture

Interestingly, respondents who served between 0–10 years ranked ministry mismatch first, while those who served between 21–30 years ranked mismatch fourth. Does this indicate that missionaries of previous generations were more flexible than more recent missionaries? Something to ponder. Notably, 'Ministry mismatch' not only features highly overall, but it is especially high amongst those serving between 0–10 years and 21–30 years, emphasising its importance.

Significantly, no matter how long missionaries served in Japan, 'God's call' to leave was highlighted, albeit in combination with other factors such as missionaries' parents' needs, lack of education options, etc. This illustrates that God's call to leave Japan is often discerned through multiple factors, as stated above.

Interview results

This section gives an overall picture of interviewees' responses. Some general comment is given after each question, but Chapter 3 provides more-detailed reflections and recommendations. (Please note that responses to some interview questions are not relevant to the focus of this book and are therefore not included. See Appendix B1 for all the questions asked in the interview.)

Why did you leave Japan?

When asked, "As you reflect on leaving Japan, talk me through why and how you came to that decision," the responses in order of popularity (the number of interviewees who mentioned the issue, rather than the number of times it was mentioned) were:

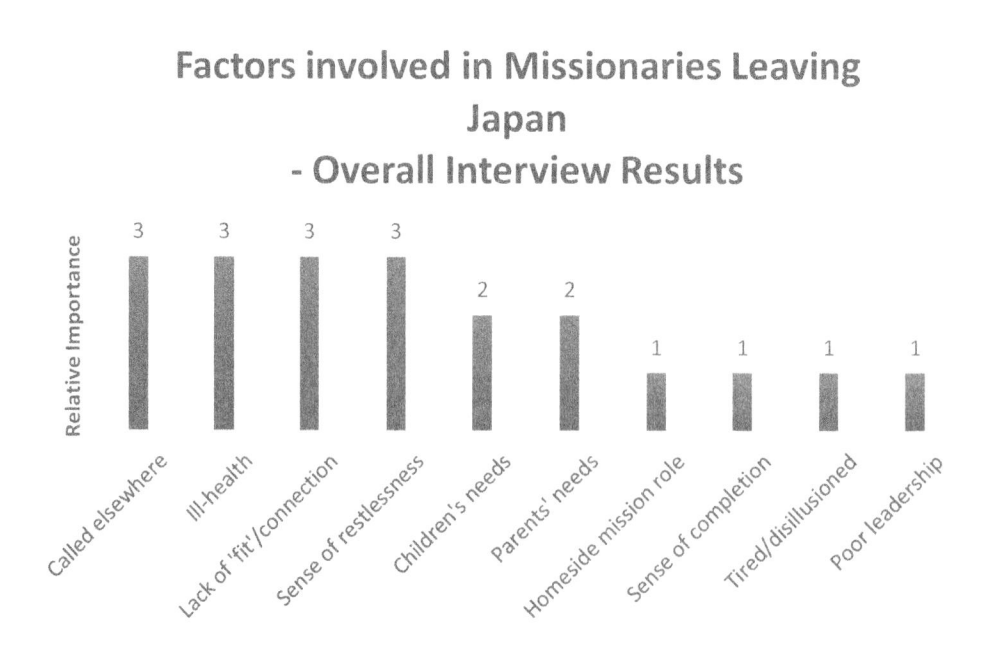

Factors involved in Missionaries Leaving Japan - Overall Interview Results

Factor	Relative Importance
Called elsewhere	3
Ill-health	3
Lack of 'fit'/connection	3
Sense of restlessness	3
Children's needs	2
Parents' needs	2
Homeside mission role	1
Sense of completion	1
Tired/disillusioned	1
Poor leadership	1

Once again, encouragingly, the primary stated reason for leaving Japan was God's call. One participant summed up, "we struggled with the decision to leave...But at the end of the day...it was really clear that the Lord had led us."

However, most interviewees gave more than one reason for leaving Japan, which shows that more often than not several factors shape missionaries' understanding of God's call to leave.[7] One participant, when asked if multiple factors were involved in their decision to leave Japan, replied, "Yeah...they all just kind of crashed down on us at once." My own parents, missionaries to the Democratic Republic of Congo in 1966–1973, left because they had trained Congolese do their roles and because I was unwell and needed schooling. These three factors culminated in their understanding of God's call to leave Congo.

Ill health, age, stress and physical and mental health problems also ranked highly.[8] For example, one interviewee commented about the months following the triple disaster of 2011 saying, "those months…were probably the hardest of my life. I didn't know how to stay in Japan as much as I loved it…anxiety issues…came to the surface to the point where I almost couldn't function."

Several interviewees identified "Lack of fit or connection with agency" as a reason why they left Japan. This parallels the survey results, in the areas of ministry mismatch and change of values, beliefs, vision and mission.

Reflecting the survey results, interviewees also ranked the needs of their children and parents highly in their reasons for leaving Japan. This further emphasises the challenges in educating and caring for missionaries' children and caring for ageing parents.

It is important to point out that the actual reasons for a missionary leaving may sometimes differ from those given by the missionary.[9] Several authors have commented on the acceptable and unacceptable 'faces of attrition', emphasising the difficulty for individuals and researchers to definitively identify reasons for departure.[10]

Although God's call ranked top in these results, some missionaries no doubt leave Japan without feeling 'called to leave', in cases like dismissal, extreme ill-health, agency mismatch and so forth. These may properly be termed attrition, since they are leaving missionary service prematurely, painfully or both.[11]

Therefore, those involved in missionary care should perhaps help 'leavers' (for whatever reason) navigate withdrawal in pastoral ways. Their aim should try to ensure that missionaries' departure is ultimately positive rather than negative, remembering that "in all things God works for the good of those who love him" (Romans 8:28, NIV).

What do you wish you had done differently?

When I asked missionaries, "What, if anything, do you wish you had done differently, either in regard to self-care on the field, or in the process of leaving?", they emphasised self-awareness and a better work/life balance. (For brevity and focus, this book does not address the process of leaving.)

One interviewee commented, "I wish I would have known my personality type…and my coping skills better. Because in the difficult times…knowing who I am now…I think I would have done things differently than how I did when I was there." It is worth remarking that although self-awareness develops naturally and supernaturally, it can be learnt, in part.

Commenting on having a better work/life balance (which could also include saying no), one participant said, "it really helps to have a good balance and…never be so busy that you don't have time for fellowship with God and…friends, prayer partners."

What do you wish your mission agency had done differently in regard to member care?

Interviewees were asked, "As you reflect on leaving Japan, what, if anything, do you wish your mission had done differently?"

The most popular answers to this question included intentional member care, home-side debriefing, and field-side debriefing.

Commenting on intentionality in member care, several interviewees said that this area had not initially been very well developed organisationally. One interviewee said "I think in our early years, member care wasn't really talked about." Another commented, "Member care was not a main focus when we started…now, our mission has a real system of how to do member care." Still another said that not only was member care more available now, but they were also more intentional about seeking out member care as an individual.

It is perhaps especially helpful to highlight the area of debriefing. Many researchers highlight the need for debriefing, with one commenting, "Debriefing is the unpacking of your emotional suitcase after a trip or project is completed. We often unpack our physical suitcase, but not the emotional one, carrying the contents or baggage with us to our next experience."[12] One interviewee commented, "Actually doing this interview…is probably the most debriefing I've had." This shows poor care on the part of the agency concerned.

Finally, one interviewee clearly expressed the pain associated with lack of finances: "The hardest thing [is] when you go from mission life and mission money…[To] really no money. It was crazy during that flip-over period…I felt like they sort of didn't dole it out, right. They just cut it off!" This provides a salutary lesson for field-side and home-side mission agencies in how to fairly support missionaries financially as they leave field service.

Summary – survey and interviews

It's important to stress that God sometimes calls missionaries to leave Japan — as respondents' answers clearly show. Not only that, there are times when it is absolutely the right thing for a missionary to leave, perhaps because they are damaging themselves, their family, their ministry and their organisation.[13] However, this book attempts to discover what hazards lie in missionaries' paths in order to do whatever is possible to stop missionaries getting to the point where leaving Japan is the only option left. What can be done to prevent people leaving 'early'?

[1] Taylor, William D. (1997) *Too Valuable to Lose*, p.92. Pasadena: William Carey Library.
[2] Ibid, p.92
[3] Ibid, p.92
[4] Ibid, p.92
[5] Carmichael, Amy. (1987) *Fragments that remain*. The Dohnavur Fellowship. CLC Publications, e-book 2013.
[6] Hay, R. et al. (2007) *Worth Keeping: Global Perspectives on Best Practices in Missionary Retention*, p.323. Pasadena, Calif.: William Carey Library
[7] See: Hale, Thomas & Daniels, Gene. (2012) *On Being a Missionary* (Revised Edition), p.408. California: William Carey Library; Bloecher, Detlef. (2005) 'Reducing Missionary Attrition (ReMAP) - what it said and what it did', p.1. Accessed on 26th May 2020 at: Microsoft Word - ReMAPI summary.doc (dmgint.de) and Pirolo, Neal. (2000) *The Reentry Team*, p.242. USA: Emmaus Road International
[8] Taylor, William D. (1997) *Too Valuable to Lose*, p.92. Pasadena: William Carey Library.
[9] O'Donnell, Kelly S. and Michele Lewis. (ed.) (1998) *Helping Missionaries Grow*, p.436. California: William Carey Library.
[10] Taylor, William D. (1997) *Too Valuable to Lose*, p.10. Pasadena: William Carey Library.
[11] Taylor, William D. (2002) 'Revisiting a Provocative Theme: The Attrition of Longer-Term Missionaries', p.67, *Missiology* 30 Issue 1, Accessed on 13th June 2018 at: http://journals.sagepub.com/doi/pdf/10.1177/009182960203000105
[12] Bosch, Brenda. (2014) *Thriving in Difficult Places: Member Care for Yourself and Others – Volume 3*, p.153. Self-Published by the author. www.thrivingmember.com
[13] Ibid, p.10

Highlighting Hazards: Workbook

This workbook contains the following four worksheets:

- Case studies
- Anonymous (personal) case study
- Identifying and addressing personal hazards
- Identifying and addressing mission agency hazards

These worksheets are designed to be used by missionaries to Japan and/or by mission agencies working in Japan. Their aim is to transform the survey and interview results given in Chapter 1 into practical action steps, to help missionaries and agencies to avoid hazards and improve their personal and organisational health.

With the obvious exception of the Identifying and Addressing Personal Hazards worksheet, these worksheets can be used by individuals or for group discussion.

Case studies

These case studies can be used individually or as part of a group. They can be discussed by missionary teams or within mission agencies in Japan. (They could also be used in the sending or supporting country amongst prayer and financial supporters, in order to help them understand the hazards facing missionaries to Japan.)

These cases studies are imaginary, but based around what the online survey and interviews identified as the top reasons why missionaries left Japan. Each case study is brief, so you don't have 'enough' information to fully understand the situation, but please use what you read to consider these questions:

- What are the potential hazards for this missionary unit?
- What might cause them to leave Japan within the next five years?
- What could you suggest that might help and support this missionary unit?
- What could you do, or what could a mission agency do, to address the hazards you've identified?

For example, the family at the end of their first term in case study 1 is likely to be tired! So what's the danger for them? How could this danger be averted?

Case study 1

A British family serving in Sapporo, mum aged 38, dad aged 40, with three children of 5, 7, and 10 years of age. They have completed initial language study and are nearing the end of their first five-year term of service, having trained with a Japanese pastor. They are considering relocating within Japan on their return from home assignment (furlough), but this is uncertain.

- What are some potential hazards for this missionary unit?
- What might cause them to leave Japan within the next five years?
- What might help and support this missionary unit?
- What could you do, or what could a mission agency do, to address the hazards you've identified?

Case study 2

An American couple (49 and 52 years of age) serving in rural church planting, having already served in Japan for 20 years. They have been asked to join their mission agency's leadership team and are considering this option, but there is no obvious leader for the church they currently lead.

- What are some potential hazards for this missionary unit?
- What might cause them to leave Japan within the next five years?
- What might help and support this missionary unit?
- What could you do, or what could a mission agency do, to address the hazards you've identified?

Case study 3

A Singaporean single female (40 years of age) serving in Kanto amongst young people and students, having served in Japan for 10 years already. She is considering whether her current ministry needs to change as she gets older, or whether it is sustainable for another term of ministry.

- What are some potential hazards for this missionary unit?
- What might cause her to leave Japan within the next five years?
- What might help and support this missionary unit?
- What could you do, or what could a mission agency do, to address the hazards you've identified?

Anonymous (Personal) Case Study (Page 1)

This anonymous (personal) case study is designed for use in a group setting, where members don't know each other well, but have sufficient trust relationships. It can be used as follows:

1) Individuals analyse their personal hazards and how to address them using the handout below.
2) Individuals then tear off the bottom part of their handout and put it in their pocket.
3) Then, in small groups, each individual folds the top half of their handout, places it in the middle, and grabs somebody else's.
4) The group then works through each person's potential hazards (anonymously) using the information provided and comes up with suggestions to address them.

(The idea is that missionary colleagues' wisdom may be greater than individual wisdom, possibly identifying problem areas that the individual hasn't thought of, as well as finding solutions or making suggestions they haven't considered.)

Circle one in each category:

Area of origin: North America/ South America/ Europe/ Africa/ Asia/ Australasia

Age: 20–30, 31–40, 41–50, 51–60, 60+

Marital status: Single/ Single with children/ Married without children/ Married with children

Missionary status: Independent/Agency

Length of time in Japan to date: Up to 2 years/ 2–4 years/ 5–10 years/ 11–20 years/ 20–30 years

Anonymous (Personal) Case Study (Page 2)

Ministries in Japan to date (select all that are appropriate):

- ☐ Church planting
- ☐ Student work
- ☐ Outreach to children/youth
- ☐ Outreach to elderly
- ☐ Outreach to business people
- ☐ Returnee ministry
- ☐ Administration
- ☐ Leadership
- ☐ Missionary Care
- ☐ Media and Arts
- ☐ Sports ministry
- ☐ Homeless ministry
- ☐ Teaching (English, Bible, etc.)
- ☐ Other ....

What potential hazards do you think you face as you seek to continue in ministry in Japan?

1 ....
2 ....
3 ....

✂ -------------------------

Addressing Hazards

What could you do to help yourself continue in ministry in Japan, as long as God wills?

1 ....
2 ....
3 ....

Identifying and Addressing Personal Hazards

This handout is for individual reflection and prayer by missionaries.

What personal hazards do you face in your ministry in Japan? (Check/tick all that apply.)

- ☐ Physical ill-health
- ☐ Mental ill-health
- ☐ Stress
- ☐ Overwork
- ☐ Low spiritual vitality
- ☐ Diet or lifestyle challenges
- ☐ Loneliness
- ☐ Marriage concerns
- ☐ Children's education issues
- ☐ Adult children's needs
- ☐ Children not coping with Japanese life
- ☐ Parents' needs
- ☐ Wider family needs
- ☐ Bureaucracy troubles
- ☐ Inadequate finance
- ☐ Fear of natural disasters
- ☐ Japanese language
- ☐ Japanese culture
- ☐ Change in vision, mission, beliefs or values
- ☐ Lack of connection with agency
- ☐ Ministry mismatch
- ☐ Location mismatch
- ☐ Issues with mission leadership
- ☐ Conflict with missionary team
- ☐ Individual conflict with another missionary
- ☐ Conflict with Japanese team
- ☐ Spiritual warfare
- ☐ Lack of results/tired/disillusioned
- ☐ Other _____

Addressing personal hazards

What practical steps could you take to address the personal hazards to ministry you've identified?

1) _____

2) _____

3) _____

4) _____

Identifying and Addressing Mission Agency Hazards

This handout can be used by individual missionaries or for group discussion, either within the same agency or amongst different agencies.

Recall some missionaries who have left or are about to leave your mission agency. What is your impression of why they have left? (Remember you don't know all the facts!) Discuss possible reasons for their leaving — without judgement and with compassion.

Do you notice any trends or patterns in why missionaries known to you, or your agency, left Japan? (For example, have several people left your agency due to what appears to be ministry mismatch or stress?) List trends/patterns here:

Discuss why this might be happening and what you and/or your mission could do to address the issues you've identified.

List practical ways your agency aims to address the reasons for leaving that you've identified.

What more could you do as an agency — and remember agencies are made up of individuals — to proactively and positively address the reasons for leaving that you've identified?

What will you do with this information?

Prayer

Chapter 2: Highlighting Health

This chapter examines factors which help missionaries stay in Japan and is based on the results from the survey and interviews. It considers a self-care plan to promote better long-term health amongst missionaries and how mission agencies may be able to foster missionary health and resilience. The chapter gives a broad overview of the survey and interview results. Therefore, it highlights only particularly significant factors; more detailed reflection and recommendations are provided in Chapter 3.

Survey results

The online survey about what helped missionaries stay in Japan was divided into five areas: personal factors, sending side factors, pre-field training factors, on-field training factors, on-field support factors (specific to their agencies) and on-field support factors (outside their agency).

The survey offered six options for each factor, ranging from '0' (unimportant) to '5' (most relevant/important).

(Appendix A2 gives information about survey participants, Appendix A3 gives overall factors which led missionaries to leave Japan, and Appendix A4 gives overall factors which help missionaries stay in Japan.)

Personal factors

This graph illustrates the relative importance of the top three personal factors that help(ed) missionaries stay in Japan. They are shown in order of overall ranking (God's call; devotional life; supportive marriage).

Personal Factors enabling Missionaries to stay in Japan

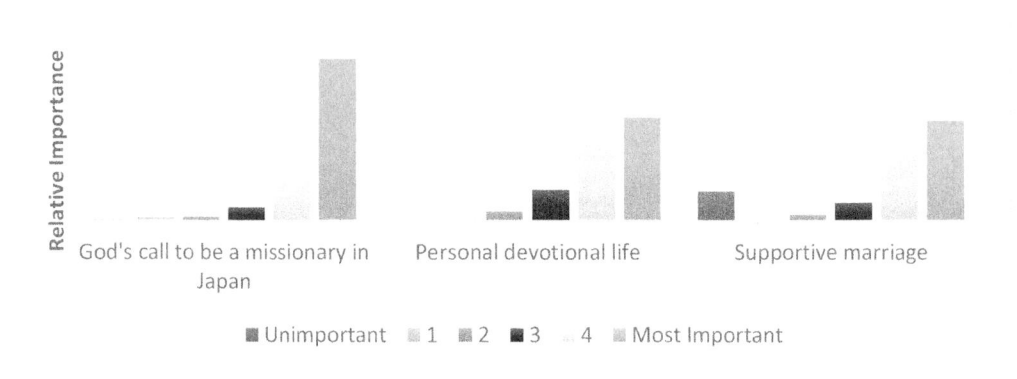

[Bar chart showing Relative Importance for three categories: God's call to be a missionary in Japan, Personal devotional life, Supportive marriage. Legend: Unimportant, 1, 2, 3, 4, Most Important]

For most participants, God's call is/was the primary personal factor that enables/enabled them to stay in Japan. This result echoes previous surveys amongst missionaries worldwide[1]. A whopping 73% of survey participants ranked it most important. One survey respondent commented, "without the assurance of God's call, I probably would have left in the first year." Another said, "Having a clear purpose and knowledge of God's leading is essential." When things are tough, assurance of and obedience to God's call are paramount. (That has certainly been true in my experience.)

God's call is followed by missionaries' devotional lives, with one respondent commenting, "many times I doubt(ed) my call and/or usefulness — at those times especially my personal relationship with Jesus was/is of utmost importance." This finding is also supported by previous surveys, which identified missionaries' spiritual life amongst the top three retention factors.[2]

Married respondents (74% of participants) highlighted the importance of a supportive marriage in helping them stay in Japan. One commentator stated that problems with marriage and family accounted for one quarter of missionary attrition, making a supportive marriage very significant.[3]

Finally, some respondents candidly said that pride or stubbornness (the fear of what others would think if they gave up) enabled them to stay in Japan, while another expressed this as the "discipline of perseverance."

Sending-side factors

Sending-side Factors enabling Missionaries to stay in Japan

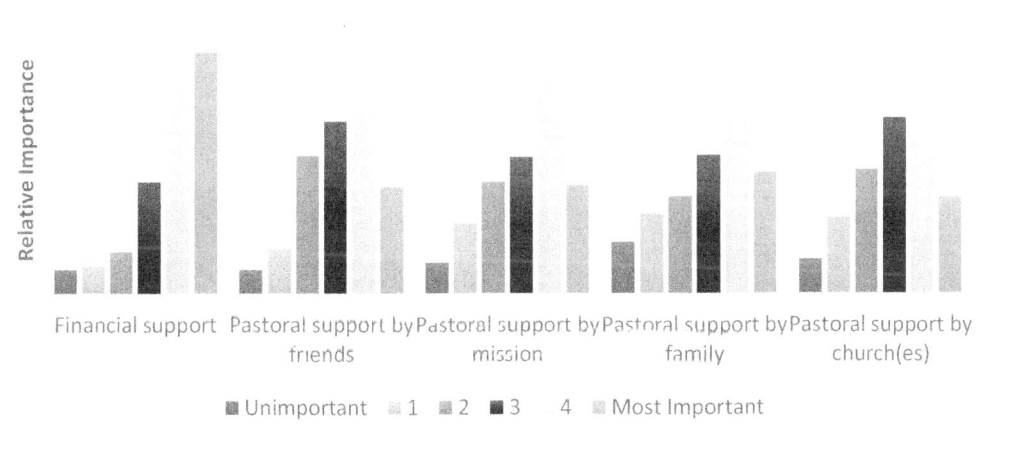

[Bar chart showing relative importance across categories: Financial support, Pastoral support by friends, Pastoral support by mission, Pastoral support by family, Pastoral support by church(es). Legend: Unimportant, 1, 2, 3, 4, Most Important]

As in other surveys, having adequate finance is linked with retention.[4] Japan has an extremely high cost of living compared with other missionary fields, so it is no surprise that financial support ranked top in this section. After all, if the money's not there, missionaries can't be in Japan!

Friends at home clearly play a vital role in providing pastoral support. This highlights the need for good communication and appropriate visits to and from home.

One respondent commented that sending-side support was particularly important at the beginning, before they had established relationships and ministry in Japan. Another participant helpfully remarked, "Financial support is necessary in that without money I could not live here. But pastoral support is important in terms of how *well* I am able to live here."

These results indicate that pastoral support by sending churches could be further developed. An effective sending side clearly helps missionaries to stay in their field of service.[5] Other commentators also identify the need for a *network* of relationships for missionaries[6], which these results also seem to support.

Other comments in this section emphasised the need for prayer by supporters and sending churches. Participants mentioned how grateful they were for such prayers, even if they didn't always know people were praying for them and their ministries.

Pre-field training factors

Pre-field Training Factors enabling Missionaries to stay in Japan

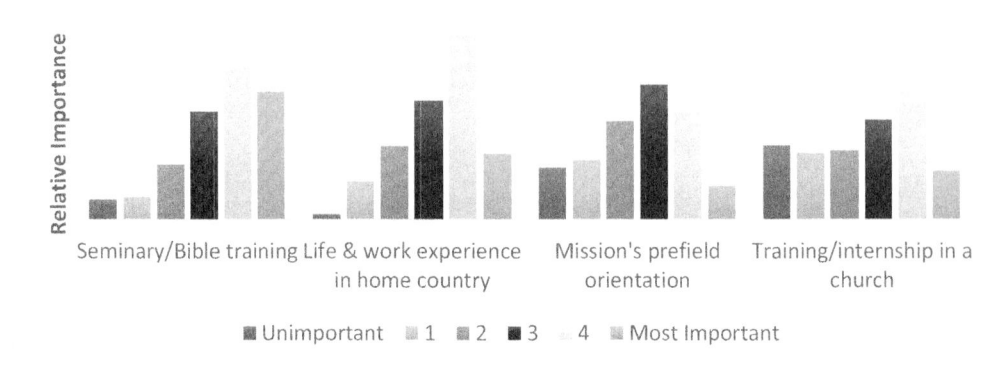

Categories (x-axis): Seminary/Bible training, Life & work experience in home country, Mission's prefield orientation, Training/internship in a church

Legend: Unimportant, 1, 2, 3, 4, Most Important

Seminary/Bible training was ranked at five by 26% of respondents and four or five by 58%. This may be due to respondents' recognition that Bible training is important for spiritual vitality and/or because most missionaries in Japan are involved in evangelism and church planting. Other studies amongst missionaries worldwide have found that higher minimal training requirements generally lead to higher retention. In other words, well-trained missionaries are likely to stay longer on the field.[7]

The high ranking of life and work experience in their home country highlights the value of home church teaching, discipling and opportunities to serve. Some respondents also mentioned the positive impact of meeting missionaries and previous short-term trips to Japan and elsewhere. Others mentioned their study of Japanese language and culture prior to missionary service helped them to stay in Japan.

On-field training factors

On-field Training Factors enabling Missionaries to stay in Japan

[Bar chart showing relative importance of: Initial language learning, Ongoing language learning, Ongoing culture learning, Initial culture learning, Ongoing training in other areas, On-field orientation. Legend: Unimportant, 1, 2, 3, 4, Most Important]

Unsurprisingly, initial language learning was ranked at five by 39% of missionaries and four or five by 73% in terms of on-field training factors that helped them stay in Japan.

Furthermore, 25% of respondents ranked ongoing language learning at five and 70% ranked it four or five. These figures and similar studies[8] show that language and culture study (both initial and ongoing) is extremely important in enabling missionaries to stay on the field. This is perhaps especially true in Japan, because of the complexity of the Japanese language and culture (see Appendix D). The Effective Language Learning website rates Japanese as the most difficult language for native English speakers to learn.[9]

Interestingly, ongoing culture learning was ranked third, above initial culture learning. This may be because when missionaries first arrive in Japan, they are so overwhelmed by learning the language that they can't see beyond it to culture. However, as they spend longer in Japan and their language ability improves, they become more aware of cultural differences and their need for ongoing culture learning.

Surprisingly, on-field orientation was ranked last (other studies have found similar results amongst missionaries[10]). This may be because new missionaries are initially so bewildered that on-field orientation, though vital at the time, is forgotten. Alternatively, as some comments suggest, it may be because some mission agencies provide insufficient or poor-quality orientation, while many non-agency respondents didn't receive any orientation at all. This area clearly merits further investigation and improvement.

Other comments mentioned the desire for training in team building, prayer, soul care, mentoring, spiritual development, and emotional intelligence. Strikingly, respondents who had served for 16 years or longer expressed increased awareness of their need for ongoing training. Commentators have noted the correlation between ongoing training and missionary retention.[11]

Finally, one person made the helpful distinction between on-field training factors that *enabled them to stay* in Japan and those that *helped them grow* in life and ministry.

On-field support factors (mission-agency specific)

On-field Agency-specific support factors enabling Missionaries to stay in Japan

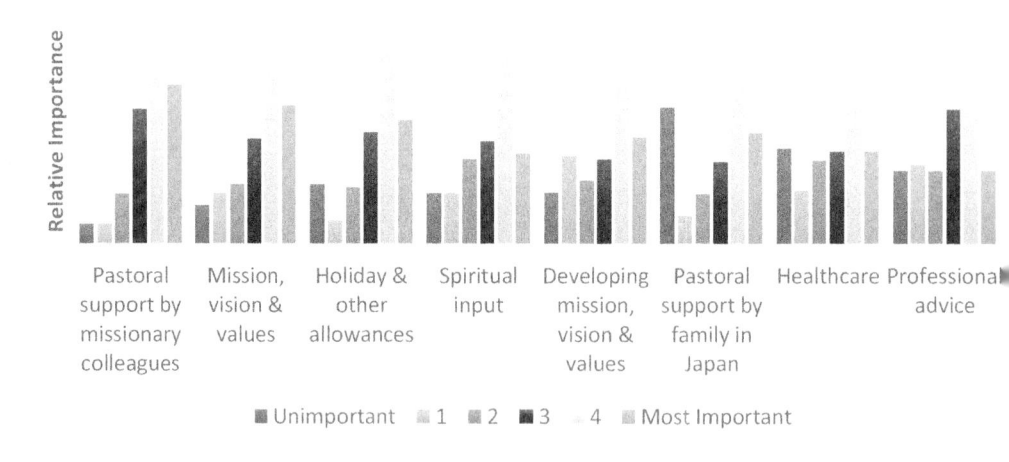

[Bar chart showing relative importance of factors: Pastoral support by missionary colleagues, Mission, vision & values, Holiday & other allowances, Spiritual input, Developing mission, vision & values, Pastoral support by family in Japan, Healthcare, Professional advice. Legend: Unimportant, 1, 2, 3, 4, Most Important]

Pastoral support by fellow missionaries was ranked top. This was borne out in the interviews and is supported by similar research into the value of supportive communities.[12]

I was surprised at how high the mission, vision, and values of agencies was ranked although other studies of missionaries around the world have observed this too.[13] This again confirms the need for agencies to be transparent during recruitment and beyond. As noted in Chapter 1, agency mismatch leads to problems and pain for both missionaries and agencies.

Furthermore, though ranked fifth, developing mission, vision, and values is similar. One commentator included this in his list of practices that boost missionary retention. He highlights organisations that seek staff suggestions and involve staff in decisions that affect them.[14] Missionaries need to be enabled and encouraged to take an active part in determining ministry priorities and operating procedures.

I think it is extremely significant that holiday/vacation and other allowances were ranked third. As discussed in Chapter 1, many people in Japan work a lot of overtime and take few holidays, and there are a high number of deaths due to overwork.[15] This result may suggest that many missionaries are too busy, perhaps finding it difficult to take time off when their Japanese colleagues don't. Moreover, I suspect many missionaries overwork because of Japan's vast spiritual need, feeling that they cannot afford to rest. This result illustrates the vital role for agencies of ensuring that their missionaries do not overwork and are given (and actually take) adequate time off. It also shows the importance of leaders setting a healthy example in this area.[16]

Ranked only slightly lower than holidays/vacation was spiritual input by the mission agency. This highlights the need for agencies to consider how to encourage their missionaries spiritually, through conferences, prayer, retreats, and so forth.

Other comments in this section included an appreciation of child care, children's education, flexibility in mission leadership, and medical care. Some survey respondents commented that their leadership didn't understand or listen, whereas others praised leaders who made decisions based on polices rather than on micro-management tendencies. Proficient leadership clearly prolongs missionary longevity, and this was also borne out in the interviews.

Finally, showing that more on-field support is still needed, one person regrettably lamented, "I wish there was an area to mark non-existent".

On-field support factors (outside agency)

On-field Non-agency-specific support factors enabling Missionaries to stay in Japan

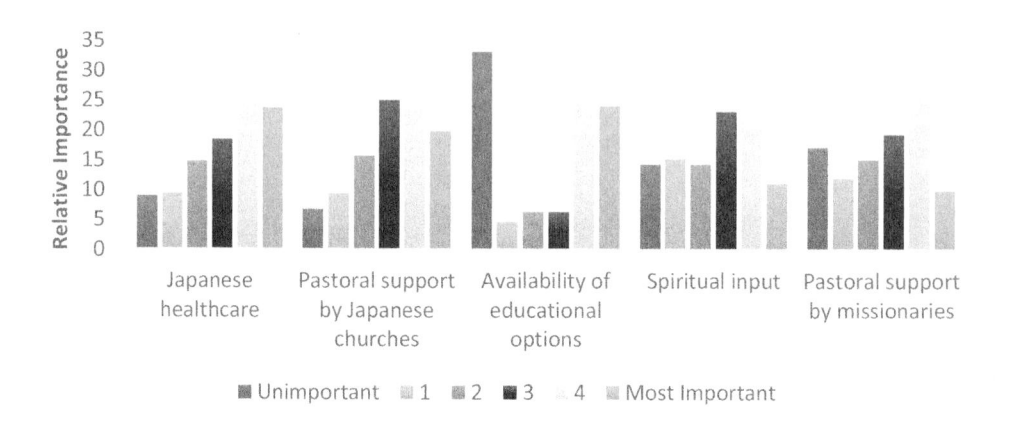

[Bar chart showing Relative Importance (0-35) across five categories: Japanese healthcare, Pastoral support by Japanese churches, Availability of educational options, Spiritual input, Pastoral support by missionaries. Each category has bars for Unimportant, 1, 2, 3, 4, Most Important.]

Other researchers[17] have noted that good healthcare improves missionary retention. It's important to recognise and give thanks to God for the Japanese healthcare system. It enables many missionaries to stay in Japan, whereas they might have had to leave the field had they been serving in countries with inferior health systems. Respondents also mentioned the benefit of sport and exercise. Encouragingly, the support of Japanese believers is highly appreciated, despite the relatively small Christian population.

The availability of educational options was ranked third overall, but survey respondents with children ranked it first. This concurs with other similar studies amongst missionaries around the world[18], showing that educational choices affect family life and ministry context and content (not to mention the child's future!). This is an important, complex issue with no easy solution, demanding a lot of thought by parents and mission agencies alike.

Survey respondents ranked spiritual input and pastoral support by missionaries outside their agencies lower, but it was encouraging to see positive mention of the Japan Evangelical Missionary Association (JEMA) and the Church Planting Institute (CPI). Was this lower ranking because missionaries received adequate support from their own agency (and/or family, friends or supporters) and so didn't need to look elsewhere? Or does it highlight the general lack of cross-agency cooperation in ministry and fellowship — with some notable exceptions? Although this gap is partially addressed by JEMA and CPI, perhaps more could be done to support missionaries across agencies. Certainly, it is an area to think about more deeply and creatively.

Overall survey results

Finally, the top-ten factors overall that enable missionaries to stay in Japan are:

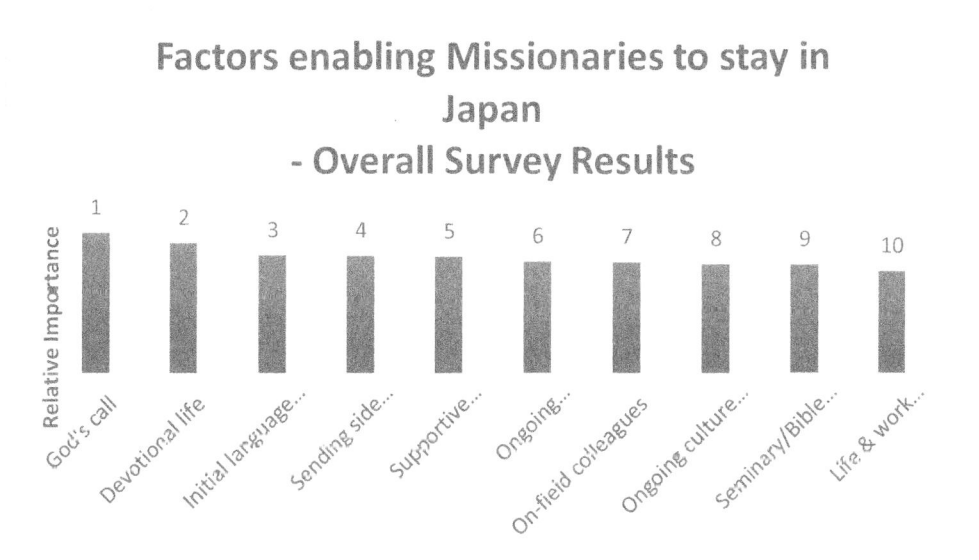

**Factors enabling Missionaries to stay in Japan
- Overall Survey Results**

Rank	Factor
1	God's call
2	Devotional life
3	Initial language...
4	Sending side...
5	Supportive...
6	Ongoing...
7	On-field colleagues
8	Ongoing culture...
9	Seminary/Bible...
10	Life & work...

(Appendix A4 gives the complete results.)

These results are one of the most important parts of this book. These factors are essential in helping missionaries stay well in Japan.

God's work in the life of the missionary is primary. No experience, training, or community can take its place. Missionaries and mission agencies must do all they can to encourage and sustain individual and corporate spirituality. The results also highlight the vital importance of language and culture study, along with seminary training. Missionaries and mission agencies under-rate any of these areas of training at their peril. Finance too plays a particularly significant part in the lives of missionaries serving in a high-living-cost country like Japan. Finally, community, both in marriage and with missionary colleagues, is important, indicating that missionaries and their agencies must nurture 'mission family' life and strive to build community with one another.

Interview Results

This section gives an overall picture of interviewees' responses. Some general comments are made after each question, while Chapter 3 provides more-detailed reflections and recommendations. (Please note that responses to some interview questions – see Appendix B1 – are not relevant to the focus of this book and are therefore not included.)

What specific personal practices or self-care have helped you stay in Japan?

Interviewees responded as follows (ranked in order):

1. Personal spiritual life
1. Christian community
1. Healthy lifestyle

2. Sense of call

3. Accountability
3. Marriage and family life
3. Home country links

4. Local community involvement
4. Helpful leadership
4. Self-awareness
4. Healthy thought life

5. Healthy ministry environment
5. Personal beliefs and values

Interviewees ranked personal spiritual life, Christian community, and a healthy lifestyle first. Personal spiritual life included personal devotions, retreats, and conferences. Christian community in both English and Japanese was important. A healthy lifestyle included things like sleeping, eating, exercise, hobbies, physical and mental health care, pets, Sabbath-keeping, and holidays.

One interviewee summed up their thoughts about the vital importance of their devotional life: "If your relationship with God is OK, then everything else is OK, even if it's rough." Other commentators have shown that missionaries' spiritual character and spiritual 'stickability' go hand in hand.[19]

Regarding the need for Christian community, one interviewee said, "(you) have (to have) people to plug into and to pray with…be able to share…struggles with…You got to have somebody." As we've seen before, missionaries benefit significantly as they experience and express community, and, once again, this has been expressed by other commentators.[20]

One participant commented about healthy lifestyle, particularly hobbies, saying, "we realized very quickly that we needed to…do things that were life giving for us." While not addressing a healthy lifestyle for missionaries directly, one author discussed self-care (caring for ourselves in every area) at length.[21]

Once again, a sense of call was extremely important, ranked second. One interviewee commented, "I guess the main thing is where God wants you. That helps you to go through a lot of patches too, doesn't it? Just knowing you feel you're where God wants you to be." One commentator says, "Calling to missionary service…is as important today for keeping missionaries on the field as it ever was."[22]

Accountability, marriage and family life, and links with the home country ranked joint third. One interviewee commented about accountability and men, "Men who struggle with whatever they struggle with, often struggle the most during transitions, because the support that they've had is not there." Others talked about the importance of having people to ask you hard questions and to be intentional in both personal and organisational accountability.

Discussing marriage and family life and maintaining links with their home country, one participant commented, "we tried to keep a real sense of family culture the same…as we have at home, as we have in Japan." However, the same person also commented, "one or two…missionaries…are kind of still so connected with their home church, that they…aren't making enough connections with people where they are." Another urged new missionaries especially to "try to detach from the home country." Yet another, however, commented on how rejuvenating returning to their home country regularly was for them. Maintaining appropriate links with the home country means different things to different people, but clearly needs to be given careful thought and planning by both individuals and agencies.

What specific practices (in regard to your organisation, if applicable) have helped you stay in Japan?

In order, the results were:

1. Member-care structures

2. Mission community

3. Good leadership

4. General reviews
4. Training and development
4. Agency retreats/conferences

5. Agency health care
5. Practical care

6. Organisational flexibility

7. Candidate processes
7. Language and orientation

Talking about member care structures, one interviewee said, "I can't but highly praise member care…I don't think we would have been…willing to call them if they hadn't been intentional and…made themselves visible." Other research amongst missionaries has highlighted the need for both proactive and reactive member-care structures.[23] That is to say, putting structures in place in advance to ensure missionaries' good care and caring for missionaries when things aren't going well.

Echoing previous research[24], the online survey results and interviewees' answers to what self-care practices helped them stay in Japan highlight the vital importance of the mission community, through regular fellowship and individual relationships. One participant said, "When I was a new missionary…coming together with English speakers…was really important, because (of) culture shock, stress, no language…not…being…fed from the Japanese context."

'Good leadership' includes things like supportive leaders, visits by leadership, and members' healthy expectations. One interviewee commented about their leaders "they were accessible. They were available. When they were present physically, they were attentive." Other commentators mentioned the need for honest and compassionate leadership, trust between leaders and staff, and having appropriate people in leadership and how essential this is in helping missionaries stay on the field.[25]

General reviews ranked fourth, but attracted important comments like, "depending on who takes the review, it can either be very encouraging or it can be quite devastating" and "the annual review was very functional and not spiritual." Plainly, it is important to conduct general reviews, but how they are done is equally important. Mission agencies must therefore give careful thought to reviews' content and timing, as well as who does them and how they are conducted.

Training and development was also ranked fourth in the interviews, similar to its ranking in the survey. Areas highlighted by interviewees for training, besides language and culture, were multicultural teams, conflict, emotional intelligence (or personal relationship skills), and cross-cultural understanding and respect. One interviewee said, "everyone is different and my own culture is not better, but it's different. When people think differently, it doesn't necessarily mean that they are not supporting you or they are not caring about you, but simply they are thinking differently."

Interviewees commented that agency retreats and conferences, also ranked fourth, were important in helping them remain on fire for God, helping them to raise their eyes from the apparent or actual lack of ministry results, and encouraging their children's spiritual life. Spiritual retreats and conferences run by mission agencies could be considered proactive member care, seeking to ensure a healthy spiritual life to help missionaries stay well in Japan.

Many of these comments emphasise that intentional, regular and deep fellowship as missionaries, leaders with members and all with one another, is one of the best things missionaries and mission agencies can do to support their members and enable them to stay in Japan. Missionaries and mission agencies must consider how to make such fellowship a priority.

What, if anything (and if applicable), would you like/have liked your mission to have done to support you more (or differently) in the area of member care?

1. Develop structures, encourage and resource member care
1. Nothing further needed

2. Agency flexibility with accountability

3. Empathetic leadership

4. Encourage a caring community
4. Develop member care for men
4. Training and development in other areas

5. Training and modelling in self-care
5. Missionary, not ministry focused

6. Introduce change gradually
6. Flatter leadership structure

Just over half (8 out of 15) the interviewees were satisfied with their agency's member care. One interviewee shared their experience of care when going through serious difficulties with one of their children, "just to think that they [the agency] were willing to do anything…we are just one family of thousands that are on the field…they made it very personal, said that… 'nothing's more important than you right now.' …that was very humbling."

However, other interviewees would like to have seen more member-care structures developed and the encouragement and resourcing of member care (including counsellors). One individual commented, "it would have been good to have more careful care…more specific care". However, another said of their organisation, "I don't know that it's a case of doing more, but how do we help people realise and access the resources that are already there?"

Commenting on agency flexibility with accountability (being able to do and say the 'tough stuff' when necessary), one interviewee pleaded with leaders to address difficult issues. He urged agencies to accept that, "if your marriage is a mess…if you're over-working, that's our [the agency's] problem." Another commented on the importance of self-discipline and routine, because as a missionary on the field there is often no one "to hold you accountable."

Finally, empathetic leadership ranked third. Ironically, this is the same ranking as in the previous question about what interviewees felt was helpful in staying in Japan. Commenting on the need for greater empathy from leaders one person said, "I would have really appreciated it if they would have taken more time to talk to us and find out how you are doing...they were very much interesting [sic] to...do sightseeing." Another observed, "I think...leadership needs a...clear idea of where they're heading...how they're going to help people, but...a basic thing is to listen." Another spoke about the possible conflicts concerning "your strategic guys and your pastoral guys", saying, "I don't think you can do that. If you don't do them together, they end up pulling in different directions and that's pretty unhelpful." One writer's comments on missionary attrition apply to mission agency leadership most of all, "Attrition isn't just bad-fit people finding the door. It is an indicator of organizational effectiveness. When agencies are well run, people stay."[26]

What advice would you give prospective and new missionaries in regard to self-care?

The overall results showed that self-care begins by choosing a pastorally responsible agency that suits the individual. With that proviso, here is the interviewees' lifestyle advice for new and prospective missionaries to Japan:

1. Find Christian community

2. Maintain personal spiritual life
2. Maintain healthy life rhythms

3. Develop self-awareness

4. Maintain a learning posture

5. Maintain home-country links appropriately
5. Be accountable
5. Remember God's supremacy

6. Be certain of God's call
6. Be respectful of others' differences

7. Get help with children

Correlating with helpful self-care practices, the main advice interviewees had for new missionaries was to find Christian community, maintain your spiritual life (including having personal devotions and attending retreats and conferences), maintain healthy life rhythms (including Sabbaths, holidays, and developing new traditions) and develop self-awareness.

Although self-awareness wasn't explicitly mentioned in the questions, interviewees raised it here and in the answers to several other questions, which makes it particularly noteworthy. One interviewee said, "self-awareness is very important; knowing yourself in relation to…God…and your identity in Jesus." Another commented, "know what works for you before you come…you don't become a different person when you come to the field…for ministry practice…as well as…how we relate to God…know yourself, know what you need."

Finally, a few comments on maintaining a learning posture. Echoing good advice he had received, one interviewee encouraged new missionaries to take time to learn about and enjoy their new environment first, before getting involved in ministry. He said, "I think some of these young people get here and they just want to hit the ground running." Another person commented on the humility every missionary needs, saying, "After arriving in Japan, I find that in fact it's me to [sic] unlearn all the things and allow myself to fail, and also acknowledging that God in fact can work through your weakness as well." A teachable attitude is vital for any missionary

Summary

Themes that emerged from the interviews include:

- the importance of God's call
- the need to maintain your spiritual life
- the centrality of Christian fellowship with both missionaries and Japanese
- the importance of healthy life rhythms
- having healthy expectations personally and organisationally
- the need to develop self-awareness
- effective and empathetic leadership
- accountability
- intentional and structured member care
- initial and continuing training

These issues are considered in greater detail in Chapter 3.

---

[1] See Fullerton, Mark A. (2010) *A Missional Reading of the Psalms of Lament: Exploring the Implications of the Lamenting Psalms as Preventative Measure for Western Missionary Attrition in the 21st Century, p.16*. Unpublished thesis: Redcliffe College; Brown, Ronald. (October-December 2006, Volume 42, Issue 4) 'Preparing for the Realities of Missions in a Changing World', Evangelical Missions Quarterly October 2006. Accessed on 9th April 2021 at: Preparing for the Realities of Missions in a Changing World - Missio Nexus and Brierley, Peter (1996) *Mission Attrition: Why Missionaries Return Home*, p.39. London: Christian Research.

[2] Hay, R. et al. (2007) *Worth Keeping: Global Perspectives on Best Practices in Missionary Retention*, p.24-25. Pasadena, Calif.: William Carey Library

[3] Brierley, Peter (1996) *Mission Attrition: Why Missionaries Return Home*, p.9. London: Christian Research.

- Missiographics. 'Going the Distance: Missionary Retention'. (No date) Accessed on 9th April 2018 at: https://visual.ly/community/infographic/lifestyle/missionary-retention; Prins, Marina & Willemse, Braam. (2002) Member Care for Missionaries, p.124. South Africa: Member Care Southern Africa and Hay, R. et al. (2007) *Worth Keeping: Global Perspectives on Best Practices in Missionary Retention*, p.340. Pasadena, Calif.: William Carey Library.
- Hay, R. et al. (2007) *Worth Keeping: Global Perspectives on Best Practices in Missionary Retention*, p.362. Pasadena, Calif.: William Carey Library.
- Brown, Ronald. (October- December 2006, Volume 42, Issue 4) 'Preparing for the Realities of Missions in a Changing World', Evangelical Missions Quarterly October 2006. Accessed on 9th April 2021 at: Preparing for the Realities of Missions in a Changing World - Missio Nexus
- Bloecher, Detlef. (2005) 'Reducing Missionary Attrition (ReMAP) - what it said and what it did', p.9. Accessed on 26th May 2021 at: Microsoft Word - ReMAPI summary.doc (dmgint.de)
- Hay, R. et al. (2007) *Worth Keeping: Global Perspectives on Best Practices in Missionary Retention*, p.120. Pasadena, Calif.: William Carey Library.
- Effective Language Learning. (2017) Accessed on: 26th December 2017 at: http://www.effectivelanguagelearning.com/language-guide/language-difficulty

[10] Hay, R. et al. (2007) *Worth Keeping: Global Perspectives on Best Practices in Missionary Retention*, p.120. Pasadena, Calif.: William Carey Library.

[11] Hay, R. et al. (2007) *Worth Keeping: Global Perspectives on Best Practices in Missionary Retention*, p.120. Pasadena, Calif.: William Carey Library and Bloecher, Detlef. (2004) 'Good Agency Practices: Lessons from ReMAP II', p.5. Connections: The Journal of the WEA Missions Commission, 3 (2), p.12-25. Accessed on 13th June 2018 at: http://worldevangelicals.org/resources/rfiles/res3_124_link_1292364866.pdf

[12] Fawcett, John. (ed.) (2003) *Stress and Trauma Handbook: Strategies for Flourishing in Demanding Environments*, p.127-128. California: World Vision International

[13] Bloecher, Detlef. (2004) 'Good Agency Practices: Lessons from ReMAP II', p.11. Connections: The Journal of the WEA Missions Commission, 3 (2), p.12-25. Accessed on 13th June 2018 at: http://worldevangelicals.org/resources/rfiles/res3_124_link_1292364866.pdf

[14] Nelson, J. (2015) 'Excellence in Missions: Four Ways to Improve Field Staff Retention', no page. *Evangelical Missions Quarterly*, Vol. 51, No. 4 pp. 440-445. Accessed on 8th June 2021 at: EMQ_Volume_51_Issue_4.pdf

[15] Lane, Edwin. (2017) 'The young Japanese working themselves to death'. Accessed on 1st January 2018 at: http://www.bbc.com/news/business-39981997

[16] Hay, R. et al. (2007) *Worth Keeping: Global Perspectives on Best Practices in Missionary Retention*, p.216. Pasadena, Calif.: William Carey Library

[17] Prins, Marina & Willemse, Braam. (2002) *Member Care for Missionaries*, p.124. South Africa: Member Care Southern Africa

[18] Van Meter, Jim. (2003) *US Report of Findings on Missionary Retention*, p.7. Accessed on 14th June 2018 at: http://www.worldevangelicals.org/resources/rfiles/res3_95_link_1292358708.pdf

[19] See Selvey, David, (2015) 'Missionary Retention'. Accessed on 9th April 2018 at: https://blogs.faithlafayette.org/missions/missionary-retention/ and Fullerton, Mark A. (2010) *A Missional Reading of the Psalms of Lament: Exploring the Implications of the Lamenting Psalms as Preventative Measure for Western Missionary Attrition in the 21st Century*, p.16. Unpublished thesis: Redcliffe College

[20] Nelson, James. (2010) 'The Engage! Study Executive Summary', *Evangelical Missions Quarterly* Volume 46:3, Accessed on 8th June 2021 at: The Engage! Study Executive Summary - Missio Nexus

[21] Bosch, Brenda. (2014) *Thriving in Difficult Places: Member Care for Yourself and Others* – Volume 2, p.199-228. Self-Published by the author. www.thrivingmember.com

[22] ReMAP II by Hay, R. et al. (2007) *Worth Keeping: Global Perspectives on Best Practices in Missionary Retention*, p.93. Pasadena, Calif.: William Carey Library

[23] Shepherd, David. L. (2014) *Promoting Missionary Mutual Care Through Spiritual Community*, p.60-61. Accessed on 7th May 2018 at: http://digitalcommons.georgefox.edu/cgi/viewcontent.cgi?article=1085&context=dmin

[24] See Nelson, James. (2010) 'The Engage! Study Executive Summary', *Evangelical Missions Quarterly* Volume 46:3, Accessed on 8th June 2021 at: The Engage! Study Executive Summary - Missio Nexus and Powell, John. R. & Bowers, Joyce. M. (2002) *Enhancing Missionary Vitality*, p.113-4. Colorado: Mission Training International

[25] Nelson, James. (2015) 'Excellence in Missions: Four Ways to Improve Field Staff Retention', Evangelical Missions Quarterly, Vol. 51, No. 4 pp.440-445 Accessed on 8th June 2021 at: EMQ_Volume_51_Issue_4.pdf

[26] Ibid, no page.

Highlighting Health: Workbook

This workbook contains the following five worksheets:

- What personal practices helped you stay in Japan?
- What mission agency practices helped you stay in Japan?
- What advice would you give new missionaries in regard to self-care?
- Personal care plan
- Mission agencies/independent missionaries: highlighting health

These worksheets are designed to be used by missionaries to Japan and/or by mission agencies working in Japan. Their aim is to transform the survey and interview results given in Chapter 2 into practical action steps, to help missionaries and agencies to improve their personal and organisational health and to stay well in Japan for as long as God calls.

With the obvious exception of the Personal Care Plan worksheet, the worksheets can be used by individuals and as a basis for group discussion.

What personal practices helped you stay in Japan?

The list below shows interviewees' ranking of personal practices which help/helped them stay in Japan. For example, 'Personal spiritual life', 'Christian community', and 'Healthy lifestyle' ranked joint first, followed by 'Sense of call'. Take time to read the list and then consider the questions below.

1) Personal spiritual life
1) Christian community
1) Healthy lifestyle
****
2) Sense of call
****
3) Accountability
3) Marriage and family life
3) Home-country links
****
4) Local-community involvement
4) Helpful leadership
4) Self-awareness
4) Healthy thought life
****
5) Healthy ministry environment
5) Personal beliefs and values

What do these results mean for individual missionaries?

How are you putting these important factors in place in your life? In what ways do you need to improve?

What do these results mean for mission agencies?

How is your agency helping missionaries put these important factors in place? How could the agency be of further help?

What mission agency practices help/helped you stay in Japan?

The list below shows interviewees' ranking of mission agency practices that help/helped them stay in Japan. For example, 'Member care structures' ranked first, followed by 'Mission community', then 'Good leadership', followed by 'General reviews', 'Training and development' and 'Agency retreats/ conferences' in joint fourth place. Take some time to read through the list and then consider the questions below.

1) Member care structures
****
2) Mission community
****
3) Good leadership
****
4) General reviews
4) Training and development
4) Agency retreats/conferences
****
5) Agency health care
5) Practical care
****
6) Organisational flexibility
****
7) Candidate processes
7) Language and orientation

What do these results mean for mission agencies?

How is your agency caring for missionaries in these ways?

How could your agency improve in these areas?

How can these results be acted upon at an agency level?

What advice would you give new missionaries in regard to self-care?

The list below shows interviewees' advice to new missionaries in regard to self-care. For example, interviewees ranked 'Find Christian community' first, followed by 'Maintain personal spiritual life' and 'Maintain healthy life rhythms' in joint second place. Take some time to read through the list and then consider the questions below.

1) Find Christian community
****

2) Maintain personal spiritual life
2) Maintain healthy life rhythms
****

3) Be self-aware and develop self-awareness
****

4) Maintain a learning posture
****

5) Maintain home-country links appropriately
5) Be accountable
5) Remember God's supremacy
****

6) Be certain of God's call
6) Be respectful of others' differences
****

7) Get help with children

As an individual missionary, what do these results imply for you as you talk with or mentor new or future missionaries?

Is there anyone you are mentoring or could mentor in these areas?

What do these results imply for mission agencies, in terms of recruitment and training for new/future missionaries?

Personal Care Plan (Page 1)

This worksheet is for individual reflection and prayer, and combines lessons from Chapters 1 and 2.

Identifying Personal Hazards (See Chapter 1 for more detail)

What personal hazards do you face in your ministry in Japan? (Check/tick all that apply)

- ☐ Physical ill health
- ☐ Mental ill health
- ☐ Stress
- ☐ Overwork
- ☐ Low spiritual vitality
- ☐ Diet or lifestyle challenges
- ☐ Loneliness
- ☐ Marriage concerns
- ☐ Children's education issues
- ☐ Adult children's needs
- ☐ Children not coping with Japanese life
- ☐ Parents' needs
- ☐ Wider family needs
- ☐ Bureaucracy troubles
- ☐ Inadequate finance
- ☐ Fear of natural disasters
- ☐ Japanese language
- ☐ Japanese culture
- ☐ Change in vision, mission, beliefs or values
- ☐ Lack of connection with agency
- ☐ Ministry mismatch
- ☐ Location mismatch
- ☐ Issues with mission leadership
- ☐ Conflict with missionary team
- ☐ Individual conflict with another missionary
- ☐ Conflict with Japanese team
- ☐ Spiritual warfare
- ☐ Lack of results/tired/disillusioned
- ☐ Other _____

Addressing Personal Hazards

What practical steps could you take to address the personal hazards to ministry you've identified?

1) _____
2) _____
3) _____

Personal Care Plan (Page 2)

Highlighting Personal Health

From the list below, which health-giving practices do you *particularly* need to focus on? (Check/tick all that apply)

- ☐ Reviewing God's call
- ☐ Deepening your devotional life
- ☐ Seeking external spiritual input
- ☐ Evaluating your life rhythms
- ☐ Arranging a holiday
- ☐ Getting a health check-up
- ☐ Developing your self-awareness
- ☐ Working at your marriage relationship
- ☐ Working at your family relationships in Japan
- ☐ Seeking community among missionaries
- ☐ Getting an accountability partner/group
- ☐ Seeking local Christian Japanese community
- ☐ Seeking local non-Christian Japanese community
- ☐ Working at your family relationships at 'home'
- ☐ Working at your relationship with your sending church
- ☐ Working at your relationship with your sending agency
- ☐ Working towards raising more financial support
- ☐ Language learning
- ☐ Culture learning
- ☐ Learning more about your agency's mission, vision and values
- ☐ Getting (more) seminary training
- ☐ Getting training in a particular area
- ☐ Getting experience in a particular area
- ☐ Getting professional advice in a particular area
- ☐ Speaking with leadership about your concerns
- ☐ Examining educational options

Implementing Personal Health Practices

What practical steps could you take to implement the personal health practices you've identified?

1) _____
2) _____
3) _____

Mission Agencies/Independent Missionaries: Highlighting Health

This worksheet is for group reflection and prayer, for missionaries and mission agencies.

1) What member care structures does your mission agency have? What member care structures are open to you at a group/organisational level, if any? Are they fit for purpose? Do you have any other suggestions?

2) How does your mission agency encourage spiritual health? In what ways can you join with others to encourage your spiritual health? Is this sufficient? What other suggestions do you have?

3) How does your mission agency promote physical and mental health? In what ways can you promote your physical and mental health through involvement with other organisations? Is this sufficient? What other suggestions do you have?

4) How does your mission agency stimulate 'community' amongst missionaries? How can you be involved in the wider missionary community? Is this sufficient? What other suggestions do you have?

5) How does your mission agency (if applicable) demonstrate organisational flexibility and good leadership? Is this sufficient? What other suggestions do you have?

6) How does your mission agency care for candidates and train new missionaries? In what ways could you educate and train yourself for ministry in Japan in partnership with other organisations? Is this sufficient? What other suggestions do you have?

7) What are you going to do with what you've discussed?

Chapter 3:

Recommendations & Reflections for Self-care & Agency Member Care

In this chapter, I reflect on the survey and interview results and related literature to make recommendations for missionaries' self-care and mission agencies' member care practices in Japan. Due to space limitations, only the most significant themes arising from the survey and interviews are explored.

God's call

Similar to previous studies of missionaries around the world[1], survey respondents (73%) and interviewees highlighted the supreme importance of God's call, both to serve in Japan and to leave Japan. One interviewee said, "Make sure you know deep in your core that God has called you to Japan, and you're not going to keep wobbling…when it gets hard." This has important implications for missionaries and agencies.

Potential missionaries should be encouraged to carefully examine and test God's call to Japan and to a particular agency (when applicable). There are different theological understandings of calling and what it means, but the survey and interview results clearly show that knowing you are where God wants you to be and doing what God wants you to do makes all the difference. One commentator says, "Ensuring a firm call at the beginning seems to contribute to resiliency."[2] Equally, agencies have a responsibility to require a clear account of an individual's leading to missionary work in Japan and to their particular agency.

It may be helpful for current missionaries to Japan to regularly reflect on God's call. This could be enabled through organisational reviews and interviews, and personal retreat and contemplation. One participant said, "It's been very hard…but we've learned to love being where God has put us."

An assurance of God's call that holds firm during dark times is needed if missionaries are to stay in Japan, or if God calls them to leave. For example, a former missionary said, "We never intended to leave…but obviously God…had other plans."

We…never regretted our decision to live and work in Japan, but neither do we regret following God's call to ***"

Spiritual life

Like previous studies of missionaries around the world[3], survey respondents (46.5% on average) and interviewees identified a vibrant spiritual life as vital to missionary retention in Japan. One interviewee commented, "Strategy's good…but…the number-one strategy is, you get your people on fire." Some authors have also highlighted the importance of spiritual formation, spiritual character, and healthy spirituality for boosting missionary retention.[4]

Prospective missionaries thus need to be spiritually mature, have cultivated personal and corporate devotional practices, and have some understanding of spiritual warfare. This could be facilitated through training in Bible, mission, spiritual formation, and self-awareness. New missionaries who are spiritually immature will struggle to feed themselves spiritually and maintain spiritual vitality in Japan's harsh spiritual climate, especially when they are undergoing transition and have low Japanese proficiency. One author commented, "Some missionaries are going to the field too early, without…the right foundation in Christ…Who you are at home is who you will be on the field, but with added stress…that widen(s) existing cracks."[5] Consequently, mission agencies must carefully assess missionary candidates' spiritual maturity, vitality, and resilience.

Moreover, all missionaries must intentionally nurture their personal and corporate spiritual life through Bible studies, small prayer groups, larger prayer meetings, conferences, retreats, and so forth. Mission agencies could also support spiritual development through regular fellowship, agency retreats and conferences, regular reviews, and policies regarding sabbaticals and leave for spiritual refreshment

Finally, missionaries and agencies need to be aware of the reality of spiritual warfare and its expressions in Japan, as well as strategies for handling it and related ministry expectations.[6] One interviewee cautioned, "always be aware that it is a battle field and…you might get…taken out if you're not careful." Furthermore, this battle can only be fought spiritually, through prayer. Missionary to China J. O. Fraser said, "I am feeling more and more that it is, after all, just the prayers of God's people that call down blessing upon the work, whether they are directly engaged in it or not. Paul may plant and Apollos water, but it is God who gives the increase; and this increase can be brought down from heaven by believing prayer, whether offered in China or in England…If this is so, then Christians at home can do as much for foreign missions as those actually on the field…What I covet more than anything else is earnest, believing prayer."[7] What Japan needs more than anything are missionaries, agencies, and supporters who pray.

Finances

Similar to previous surveys on missionary attrition in a global context[8], insufficient financial support was ranked fourth overall by survey respondents amongst reasons for leaving Japan. As mentioned in Chapter 2, this is unsurprising considering Japan's high cost of living. However, interestingly, interviewees rarely mentioned finances, although one did say they had been "damaged" by the unhelpful financial policies of their mission agency after leaving Japan.

Several authors have discussed missionary finances. One identified finances as one of missionaries' top-ten stressors[9], while others cited irresponsible finances as a cause of attrition, which could be prevented if handled appropriately.[10]

Agencies thus have a duty of care to develop clear, pastoral financial policies, which set realistic budgets for missionaries living in Japan. Agencies also need to communicate these policies and the rationale behind them to prospective and current missionaries and supporters. In my experience, agencies are often under pressure to reduce costs. However, if that means missionaries cannot afford adequate, comfortable housing or to eat healthily or to take sufficient holidays (vacations), the agency is not fulfilling its duty and it could lead to missionaries leaving Japan. Given Japan's high cost of living, it may be beneficial for agencies to provide advice and training in this area. This could help missionaries develop and maintain financial partners and live inexpensively in Japan. It may also be valuable to provide cheap holiday homes (possibly in partnership with other agencies).

Missionaries, on the other hand, have a responsibility to live prudently yet generously and to communicate regularly and openly with their financial supporters.

Family life

The survey and interview results clearly indicate the importance of family, both as a cause of why missionaries leave Japan and as something that helps them to stay in Japan. Below, I consider family life by reflecting on marriage, children, singles, and parents.

Marriage

Marriage was identified amongst the top-five retention factors by survey respondents, and its importance was emphasised by interviewees. Moreover, previous surveys amongst missionaries around the world identified marriage or family conflict among the top-ten reasons for missionary attrition.[11]

Therefore, mission agencies should evaluate married candidates' relationships, encouraging (or requiring) them to take remedial action if needed, before coming to Japan. New missionaries are under great stress, and their marriages must be strong enough to cope.

Additionally, married missionaries need to be deliberate in spending time together, engaging in spiritual disciplines, leisure activities, and some kind of marriage enrichment. Since healthy marriages aid retention, it naturally follows that unhealthy marriages strain, and can even destroy, life and ministry. Mission agencies could nurture marriages through offering resources and marriage-enrichment courses and seminars in Japan, encouraging couples to participate in such events during home assignment or furlough and by considering how to offer marriage counselling, on and off the field, when necessary. Mission agencies would also be wise to formulate marriage- and family-affirming policies; for example, regarding the maximum time spouses may be apart annually.

Children

Of married respondents, 87% had children, highlighting the vital need for member care for families.

Children's education and the needs of adult children were among the top-ten attrition factors in the survey and were also mentioned by interviewees. One author noted that raising children cross-culturally is one of the main areas that missionaries seek help in.[12]

In regard to education, modern missionaries seem to prefer the freedom to make their own choices rather than slot into the one-size-fits-all pattern, which is how things used to be according to some participants. Ironically, more choice may mean fewer options, as some options may become unworkable. For example, in previous generations, many of OMF Japan's missionary children attended OMF's Chefoo School in Hokkaido. However, as education choices expanded, more missionaries chose local Japanese education, in-country international schools (like the Christian Academy of Japan), or international schools overseas (like Hebron School in India). Consequently, fewer children attended Chefoo School, leading to its eventual closure. As a practical outworking of this, one interviewee said, "we had a…German school, but it finished before our children started … so what are we going to do [sic]?"

Agencies, therefore, continually need to address the availability of — and even pioneer — educational options, but this is not straightforward. Van Ochs, however, provides a helpful perspective: "the pendulum has…swung in the direction of caring for… the family…. This isn't a commentary on the 'cult of the family,'…. It is merely an observation that people feel like terrible parents when their kids don't turn out to be the wonderfully well-adjusted, trilingual, Rhodes scholar MKs." [13]

In Chapter 1, I noted how frequently the needs of adult children (ranked tenth overall) contributed to missionaries leaving Japan. I have not found specific mention of this in other literature on missionary attrition. One interviewee spoke of their children's struggles to settle in their passport country. Is this just a symptom of our modern society (for example, the proliferation of anxiety and mental-health-related issues amongst young adults, the high cost of living, and so forth)? Or is it due to 'helicopter parenting', insufficient childhood attention (as one interviewee sadly confessed), or the more recent pattern of shorter, more frequent home assignments? Or is it an inevitable part of the missionary-kid experience?

Overall, the survey and interview results highlight the absolute necessity of all-round care for missionary kids of every age. Therefore, agencies should consider how they can offer educational advice and support, address adjustment issues with parents, and help parents develop family time (both before and during their time in Japan). Missionaries, meanwhile, must consider how best to educate each child, as well as how to proactively facilitate their adjustment to Japan *and* their passport country.

Singles

Singles accounted for one third of survey respondents. Several highlighted the importance of supportive friendships, which corroborates the importance of community. Without adequate support, single missionaries may be especially vulnerable to attrition. However, loneliness (which is not limited to singles) was ranked only 17th amongst reasons for leaving. Other writers, though, have highlighted loneliness and isolation as factors in missionary attrition.[14] It is thus critical that agencies help single missionaries (in particular) develop and maintain supportive relationships with other singles, families, and their local community. Meanwhile, single missionaries must be responsible and intentional in establishing and maintaining deep friendships in Japan — not just with other singles, but with couples and families too.

Parents

The needs of missionaries' parents were among the top-five reasons for leaving Japan in the survey and were raised by interviewees. A key question for missionaries is whether their family is provided for, including their parents.[15] One author wrote, "I would urge that we in the mission world intentionally seek to honour our parents and ensure they are cared for. This is an integral part of our mission — neither a liability nor a detour. Even from on the cross Jesus had "elder member care" on His mind. He said 'behold your son — behold your mother' (John 19:25–27)."[16]

The longer missionaries are in Japan, the more the issue of caring for elderly parents is likely to arise. Supporting parents fully would necessitate leaving Japan, but perhaps missionaries, mission agencies, and supporting churches could consider creative ways to care for parents from a distance. Similar to the US Family and

Medical Leave policy [17], perhaps mission agencies could consider releasing missionaries for two or three weeks of annual family leave to care for parents, or indeed other family situations as necessary. That may enable missionaries to remain in Japan, rather than forcing them to choose between the ministry they feel called to and their parents, whom they are commanded to honour. Several survey respondents left Japan to care for parents (though some had subsequently returned).

This area is especially important for older missionary candidates (since their parents will generally be older) and candidates with Asian backgrounds (since Asian cultures tend to place a particularly high value on parental care).

Missionaries should discuss care needs with their parents and siblings and seek to establish care plans if their parents are elderly or ailing. Such plans might include things such as finding someone who could check on their parents or take them to hospital and hiring a cleaner or gardener. While these things would increase support costs for missionaries, they may bring peace to both the missionary and their parents and enable missionaries to stay in Japan longer.

Language and culture learning

Initial language learning, ranked third overall, is essential for missionary retention in Japan. Furthermore, ongoing language and culture study were both ranked in the top-ten factors that help missionaries stay in Japan. Meanwhile, struggles with Japanese language featured in the top-ten reasons for leaving.

A previous survey of missionaries around the world ranked language and cultural adaptation fourth in ways to reduce missionary attrition.[18] One author commented, "effective cross-cultural ministry... requires... understanding... the customs, thinking and beliefs of the host culture."[19]

The survey results and interviewees' comments regarding challenges relating to language and culture demonstrate how essential it is to prioritise learning Japanese (especially at the beginning) and for agencies to make this possible. Moreover, mission agencies need to educate and encourage candidates and their sending churches to value language study as ministry. Agencies should educate home churches and supporters about the complexity of the Japanese language (see Appendix D about the Japanese context) and the consequent high stress levels that missionaries may well experience while learning it.

Therefore, I suggest that new missionaries to Japan should resist the temptation to focus more on external ministry than study and devote an initial period exclusively to language study. The results also highlight the value of ongoing language study, and thus missionaries and agencies must intentionally pursue this throughout a missionary's service in Japan.

In addition, the need to study Japanese culture is clear, perhaps particularly towards the end of initial language learning and beyond. Appropriate enculturation, not simply language learning, is needed if we are to reach the hearts of Japanese people.[20] Moreover, missionaries should study Japanese culture from a self-care perspective; the more they understand the culture, the more comfortable they will be living in it and be able to enjoy it. Mission agencies may want to consider establishing 'culture workshops' for new missionaries, independently or collaboratively with other agencies, which could be accessed locally or remotely.

Christian community

The need for Christian community ranked second in interviewees' advice to new or prospective missionaries and for self-care. Below, I reflect on the need missionaries have for sending-side, missionary, and local Christian communities. One author said, "Resilience rests, fundamentally, on relationships,"[21] while another commented, "God created us for…community."[22]

Sending-side community

A healthy sending-side Christian community is indispensable for missionaries. They need satisfying relationships with their sending church, mission agency, family and friends at home, and financial supporters.

Several interviewees emphasised the value of links to their home or sending countries. For example, one mentioned the need for friends and mentors from home, especially at the beginning of missionary service. Another mentioned financial provision for an annual trip home, while one talked about needing an "America fix" in order to remain in Japan. Still another pointed out the value of a supportive home-side mission.

To promote this supportive community, it is important for mission agencies to try to engage sending churches in candidate selection and pastoral support. Occasionally, sending churches may provide inadequate pastoral care, possibly because of historical patterns where only agencies provided care, an ignorance of care needs, the low 'visibility' of missionaries, and a parochial mission mind set. For example, overseas missionaries may be regarded no differently from local missionaries, whereas they need different pastoral support because they operate in another language and culture, away from usual support structures. Mission agencies would thus do well to educate and train sending churches in missionary pastoral care.

Mission agencies may also want to consider how to support missionaries in establishing and maintaining good relationships and helpful communication practices (e.g. prayer letters, visits, and using communication tools such as Skype, Zoom, and WhatsApp). Ideally, this process should begin before arrival in Japan and be reviewed regularly. Simultaneously, missionaries' self-care must include regular, appropriately open, communication with supporters, family and friends, that is neither too frequent nor too sparse.

Missionary community

Support by missionary colleagues was one of the top-ten factors in the survey for helping missionaries stay in Japan. Interviewees also emphasised the need for Christian community, with both other missionaries and Japanese Christians. One advised, "try and develop a friendship with at least one other missionary…or someone that you can relate to…take the time…to develop that relationship…it is a personal discipline." Several authors have stressed the importance of community. For example, one correlated "good community life" with retention[23]; another placed good relationships with colleagues in his list of retention factors[24], and yet another described "sturdy relationships" between missionaries as vital.[25]

Support from colleagues is critical for new missionaries who have recently left their familiar support networks, but it is also important for longer-serving missionaries. This is especially true for those living in more isolated areas, those who have moved to new locations, and single missionaries.

Although supportive friendships develop organically, mission agencies must consider how to facilitate and encourage opportunities for missionaries to get to know one another. Such 'sturdy relationships' can grow through regular fellowship (online and in person), visits to and from other missionaries, and by placing missionaries in teams.[26] Mission agencies should aim to establish a caring community through 'mission family' time and perhaps through basic training in member care for every missionary.

On the other hand, because friendships develop organically, self-care demands that missionaries be proactive in reaching out to colleagues. Some missionaries I know who rarely spent time with colleagues out of busyness, shyness, or a lack of desire are no longer in Japan (although this isn't always the case). In contrast, those who value and intentionally build community are more likely to remain. Building deep relationships takes time and money, and it may feel risky, but retention can be threatened if community is not prioritised.

Local communities

Interviewees, and to some extent survey respondents, highlighted the need to establish satisfying communities of local Christians (and non-Christian friends). One interviewee commented, "the longer I've been in Japan, [the] more of the communal elements of my faith have been able to shift to a Japanese context. I still appreciate the English context…but I'm able to, both through Japanese sermons and interactions with Japanese Christians, be encouraged."

Training

Training (pre-field, on-field, and ongoing) was slightly less emphasised, but it is worth mentioning briefly here.

Overall, Bible/seminary training ranked ninth out of 22 factors. Previous surveys of missionaries worldwide have shown that mission agencies with a good reputation for retaining missionaries in the long term commonly have higher Bible/seminary training requirements for candidates.[27] One writer commented, "Good practice agencies expect well-trained mission candidates."[28] Thus, mission agencies should require candidates to have Bible and missions training. Such training is a key prerequisite for serving in Japan as it benefits missionaries' self-care, spiritual vitality, effectiveness, and evangelistic focus.

Survey respondents who had spent 16 years or longer in Japan expressed a greater awareness of their need for ongoing training in relevant areas; six of the interviewees mentioned it 12 times. Suggestions for further training included team building, conflict resolution, stress reduction, boundaries, and spiritual warfare. One author confirmed that "good practice agencies… provide their missionaries with opportunities for continuous training and development of new gifts."[29] Other commentators have also emphasised the connection between ongoing training and reduced attrition levels.[30] Therefore, mission agencies should factor in this desire and need for ongoing training and take steps to encourage and enable lifelong learning, both in Japan and overseas and both within and outside their mission agency. Missionaries, for their part, must be intentional about acquiring further training as needed.

Competent leadership

Eight interviewees mentioned the value of good leaders 30 times! Five interviewees talked about their desire for leaders who are empathetic, flexible, good listeners, competent, and bold. These attributes were mentioned 20 times. Interviewees wanted leaders they could be accountable to, but in a 'flatter' leadership structure. One survey participant commented on leaders' flexibility, "Having…on-field leadership allowing us to pursue things God called us to do even when it meant doing the unusual. Having freedom to use the gifting we have. Having…leadership value each individual and make decisions based on broad policies rather than micromanage."

One author commented, "Good practice agencies…have effective leadership… good interaction with…missionaries, a lean quality-administration with a servant attitude and flexible structures…They encourage…missionaries to…work towards the continuous improvement of…their agency's operations and structures. Good practice agencies do not impose…changes from the top…They utilise the expertise and insight of their missionaries."[31] Another writer has highlighted the need for trust and compassion between missionaries and leaders.[32]

Therefore, competent mission leadership is vital for missionary retention. Conversely, poor leadership is damaging to individuals and ministry and can lead to attrition. Consequently, general and organisation-specific leadership training is essential; missionaries and mission agencies must consider how to achieve this. Agencies must also consider how to build empathetic yet accountable relationships between leaders and missionaries (with both sides being willing to apologise when mistakes are made, as they will be) and how to involve missionaries in setting direction.

Self-awareness and self-care

The most unexpected, but enlightening, issue raised during interviews was self-awareness. In interviewees' advice to prospective or new missionaries to Japan self-awareness ranked third, with six interviewees mentioning it 20 times. Amongst former missionary interviewees, two wished they had been more self-aware mentioning it 11 times. One bemoaned, "I wish we'd…had a deeper insight to ourselves." Another requested more training in self-awareness. Comments included, "It's not just IQ, but EQ (emotional intelligence quotient)" and "know what works for you before you come."

Linked with self-awareness, character and spiritual formation have been highlighted by one commentator as factors that encourage missionaries to stay long term.[33] Therefore, missionaries and mission agencies must consider how to develop character and self-awareness. In part, this can be achieved through varied life and ministry experience, which may mean more attention should be given to these areas during candidacy. However, self-awareness can also be developed through self-reflection and tools such as the Myers–Briggs type indicator, the DISC personality test, StrengthsFinder assessment, Enneagram, and the Sacred Pathways assessment.[34] Such training should begin during Bible and missionary training, but opportunities for reflection and learning should be ongoing.

Related to self-awareness, is self-care. For example, in regard to reasons for leaving Japan, stress (highlighted by other commentators on missionary life[35]) was ranked sixth and overwork ninth by survey respondents. One author has commented, "the struggle to do all that was apparently expected …seemed to be too great. There was too much to do, too many demands on the worker."[36]

Moreover, physical ill-health ranked fourth, mental ill-health 12th, and disillusionment 14th. On the positive side, holiday/vacation was rated as the 12th most important factor for helping missionaries stay long term. In addition, 12 interviewees mentioned a healthy lifestyle more than 50 times, and in interviewees advice to new missionaries seven recommended a healthy lifestyle more than 30 times! Several writers have also stressed the importance of self-care.[37]

Therefore, seminaries and mission agencies should train and empower prospective and current missionaries in self-awareness and to live a healthy lifestyle, which includes physical, mental, emotional, and vocational health. When discussing Sabbath-taking, one interviewee said, "I think…leaders could have modelled it better." Mission agencies urgently need to address missionary busyness, with leaders demonstrating self-care. One survey respondent commented on the inability for missionaries to take a real break due to a lack of vacation cover. While understandable, this is unhelpful in sustaining long-term ministry. Agencies have a duty of care to provide adequate leave for missionaries, including holiday/vacation, sabbatical, and family leave.

However, missionaries themselves should take heed; mission agencies can only facilitate. Missionaries should get training in self-awareness and self-care, and must prioritise and practice it. A healthy lifestyle (self-care) alone won't solve all the problems related to missionaries staying well in the longer term. However, it will help missionaries to cope with high stress levels, in a country where language and culture are particularly challenging, overwork is prevalent, and ministry disillusionment is high

Member-care structures

The positive contribution of member-care structures was mentioned more than 15 times by ten interviewees. However, defining what different individuals mean by member-care structures can be challenging. Those I interviewed referred to member-care structures as:

- candidate processing
- conferences/retreats
- regular reviews
- regular fellowship
- holiday/vacation homes
- flexibility
- training
- help in family crises
- visits by leadership for accountability and pastoral care

Commentators on missionary member-care structures include things like annual reviews, complaints procedures, risk assessment, contingency planning, and debriefing.[38] They also highlight the need for both crisis care (how to support missionaries when difficulties come) and preventative care (how to care proactively to reduce the need for crisis care).[39]

Consequently, mission agencies need to develop preventative and reactive (crisis) member care, in all its breadth and at every stage of missionaries' lives and ministries. Mission leaders are responsible for more than simply vision and mission; they are responsible for member care. One author helpfully stated, "Member care is not a department added on…but a characteristic feature that determines the overall operations: a shepherd's heart."[40] Missionaries, meanwhile, need to know their agency's member-care plan and allow themselves to be cared for and to care for others.

Suggesting improvements to mission member-care structures, one interviewee raised the possibility of on-field counsellors. Another insightfully pointed out, "I think, there's room for growth in how to engage type-A males…the types that tend to be…driven." He encouraged leaders to have the "willingness to be blunt about it," when sensing that someone was struggling. One writer commented that "self-sufficient, entrepreneurial workers tend to stuff problems and not reveal their deeper needs."[41] Another interviewee proposed men-only conferences and retreats, suggesting that agencies need to consider how to better engage men in self-care. Finally, another commented on the need to nurture a mutually caring missionary community, particularly in light of Japan's endemic busyness.

Accountability was mentioned several times by interviewees. This suggests that it would be helpful for mission agencies to encourage missionaries to develop personal accountability relationships, while also facilitating accountability in areas such as spirituality, family, mission goals and so forth, as a component of member-care structures. For example, one agency requires new missionaries to have an accountability partner before leaving for the field in order to address the issue of personal accountability.[42]

Mission 'fit'

Finally, both survey and interview results established the importance of mission 'fit' and likeminded ministry values or emphases, with 'ministry mismatch' ranking fifth overall among reasons for leaving. One commentator also mentioned the agency's role in missionary attrition, through dissatisfaction, poor communication and so forth.[43]

Therefore, agencies need to be clear and honest in communicating their mission, vision, and values during recruitment, enabling potential candidates to make informed decisions.[44] It is tempting — due to Japan's great need for the gospel — to gloss over agency specifics (like leadership or decision-making styles, for example) and accept anyone with a heart for Japan. However, there is no value — and indeed, significant potential hurt and disruption — in recruiting candidates who don't 'match' the agency.[45] OMF Japan often asks candidates why they want to come to Japan with OMF specifically, as opposed to another agency. Moreover, agencies must also make sure that they exhibit their stated values in everyday mission practice on the field; that is, not saying one thing during recruitment but behaving differently in Japan.

For their part, prospective missionaries must take responsibility to investigate different agencies and be clear about the organisation they are joining and why. Unless missionaries are well aligned with an agency's beliefs, values, mission, and vision — even simply their way of doing things — they are storing up trouble for the future. Consequently, it may be valuable for candidates to talk to missionaries already in Japan with their proposed agency, either online or through a vision trip. This may serve to reduce attrition due to mismatch, as well as smooth the transition once new missionaries arrive in Japan.[46]

However, ministry or mission mismatch can develop over time. This means that missionaries should periodically review their expectations and vision and hold prayerful discussions with leaders, perhaps through annual or biannual reviews. Survey results suggest that if missionaries stay beyond 15 years, there is a high probability they may stay 20 years or more. Therefore, I suggest that agencies need to consider how to keep more-experienced missionaries engaged, stimulated, and encouraged in ministry. This may help to extend their ministries, in line with God's call on their lives.

Mission and ministry mismatch lead to unfulfilled expectations, disillusionment, and, ultimately, departure. Therefore, clear expectations, job descriptions, and communication about these matters, including involving missionaries in developing an agency's mission and vision, is vital.

Related to this is the sense of a lack of connection with an agency, which was highlighted by the survey results. Mission agencies need to forge connections through things like more regular and/or deeper fellowship (online and/or in person) and increased staff engagement.[47]

See Brierley, Peter (1996) *Mission Attrition: Why Missionaries Return Home – Appendix Tables*, p.39. London: Christian Research; Hay, R. et al. (2007) *Worth Keeping: Global Perspectives on Best Practices in Missionary Retention*, p.24-25. Pasadena, Calif.: William Carey Library; Selvey D. (2015) 'Missionary Retention', no page. Accessed on 9th April 2018 at: https://blogs.faithlafayette.org/missions/missionary-retention/; Nelson, J. (2010) 'The Engage! Study Executive Summary', *Evangelical Missions Quarterly* Volume 46:3, Accessed on 8th June 2021 at: The Engage! Study Executive Summary - Missio Nexus

[2] Brown, Ronald. (October- December 2006, Volume 42, Issue 4) 'Preparing for the Realities of Missions in a Changing World', *Evangelical Missions Quarterly* October 2006. Accessed on 9th April 2021 at: Preparing for the Realities of Missions in a Changing World - Missio Nexus

[3] ReMAP II by Hay, R. et al. (2007) *Worth Keeping: Global Perspectives on Best Practices in Missionary Retention*, p.24-25. Pasadena, Calif.: William Carey Library

[4] See Prins, Marina & Willemse, Braam. (2002) *Member Care for Missionaries*, p.124. South Africa: Member Care Southern Africa; Selvey D. (2015) 'The Truth of Missionary Attrition, no page. Accessed on 12th June 2018 at: https://blogs.faithlafayette.org/2015/10/24/the-cost-of-missionary-attrition/

[5] Bosch, Brenda. (2014) *Thriving in Difficult Places: Member Care for Yourself and Others – Volume 1*, p.273. Self-Published by the author. www.thrivingmember.com

[6] See Mehn, John Wm. (2017) *Multiplying Churches in Japanese Soil*, p.17-24. (Pasadena: William Carey Library); and Lewis, David. C. (1993) *The Unseen Face of Japan*, p.287-290. (UK: Monarch)

[7] Taylor, Geraldine. (1998) *Behind the Ranges: The Life-changing Story of J.O. Fraser*, p.52. Singapore: OMF International (IHQ) Ltd.

[8] Brierley, Peter. (1996) *Mission Attrition: Why Missionaries Return Home– Appendix Tables*, p.39. London: Christian Research

[9] Bosch, Brenda. (2014) *Thriving in Difficult Places: Member Care for Yourself and Others – Volume 1*, p.13. Self-Published by the author. www.thrivingmember.com

[10] Steffen, Tom & McKinney Davis, Lois. (2008) *Encountering Missionary Life and Work*, p.34. Grand Rapids Michigan: Baker Academic

[11] Taylor, William D. (2002) 'Revisiting a Provocative Theme: The Attrition of Longer-Term Missionaries', *Missiology* 30 Issue 1, p.72. Accessed on 13th June 2018 at: http://journals.sagepub.com/doi/pdf/10.1177/009182960203000105

[12] Shepherd, David. L. (2014) *Promoting Missionary Mutual Care Through Spiritual Community*, p.32. Accessed on 7th May 2018 at: http://digitalcommons.georgefox.edu/cgi/viewcontent.cgi?article=1085&context=dmin

[13] Van Ochs, B. (2001) 'Ten Challenges That May Make Going Home Look Attractive', *Evangelical Missions Quarterly*, no page. Accessed on 9th April 2021 at: Ten Challenges That May Make Going Home Look Attractive - Missio Nexus

[14] Powell, John. R. & Bowers, Joyce. M. (2002) *Enhancing Missionary Vitality*, p.103. Colorado: Mission Training International

[15] Nelson, James. (2010) 'The Engage! Study Executive Summary', *Evangelical Missions Quarterly* Volume 46:3, Accessed on 8th June 2021 at: The Engage! Study Executive Summary - Missio Nexus

[16] David, R. (2019) 'Editorial: Elder Member Care', Global Member Care Network (GMCN) March 2019. Accessed on 7th May 2020 at: https://www.facebook.com/groups/globalmembercare/

[17] U.S. Department of Labor. (No date) Family and Medical Leave Act, no page. Accessed on 26th May 2021 at: Family and Medical Leave (FMLA) | U.S. Department of Labor (dol.gov)

[18] Bloecher, Detlef. (2005) 'Reducing Missionary Attrition (ReMAP) - what it said and what it did', p.6. Accessed on 26th May 2021 at: Microsoft Word - ReMAPI summary.doc (dmgint.de)

[19] Selvey, David. (2015) 'The Truth of Missionary Attrition', no page. Accessed on 12th June 2018 at: https://blogs.faithlafayette.org/2015/10/24/the-cost-of-missionary-attrition/

[20] Hay, R. et al. (2007) *Worth Keeping: Global Perspectives on Best Practices in Missionary Retention*, p.108. Pasadena, Calif.: William Carey Library

[21] Kent, Martha, Davis, Mary. C, Reich, John. W. (ed.) (2014) *The Resilience Handbook: Approaches to Stress and Trauma*, p.199. New York & London: Routledge (quoting Luthar, 2006; 2014)

[22] Wilson, Michael Todd and Hoffman, Brad. (2007) *Preventing Ministry Failure*, p.44. Illinois: IVP

[23] Nelson, James. (2015) 'Excellence in Missions: Four Ways to Improve Field Staff Retention', *Evangelical Missions Quarterly Vol. 51, No. 4* pp.440-445 Accessed on 8th June 2021 at: EMQ_Volume_51_Issue_4.pdf

[24] Bloecher, Detlef. (2005) 'Reducing Missionary Attrition (ReMAP) - what it said and what it did', p.6. Accessed on 26th May 2021 at: Microsoft Word - ReMAPI summary.doc (dmgint.de)

[25] Brown, Ronald. (October- December 2006, Volume 42, Issue 4) 'Preparing for the Realities of Missions in a Changing World', Evangelical Missions Quarterly October 2006. Accessed on 9th April 2021 at: Preparing for the Realities of Missions in a Changing World - Missio Nexus

[26] Dodds, Lois. A. & Dodds, Lawrence. E. (1999) 'Love and Survival: In Life, In Missions', p.5-9. (Part of Collected Papers on the Care of Missionaries 2000) Pennsylvania: Heartstream Resources

[27] Bloecher, Detlef. (2004) 'Good Agency Practices: Lessons from ReMAP II'. Connections: The Journal of the WEA Missions Commission, 3 (2), p.3. Accessed on 13th June 2018 at: http://worldevangelicals.org/resources/rfiles/res3_124_link_1292364866.pdf

[28] Bloecher, Detlef. (No date) 'Good agency practices – lessons from ReMAP II', p.8. Accessed on 26th May 2021 at: Good Agency Practices: Lessons from ReMAP II - Missio Nexus

[29] Ibid, p.8.

[30] See Koteskey, Ron. (2011) 'What Missionaries Ought to Know about Premature Departure from the Field'. Wilmore, Ken.: New Hope International Ministries. Accessed on 9th April 2018 at: http://www.missionarycare.com/attrition.html and Stetten, Tom & McKinney Davis, Lois. (2008) *Encountering Missionary Life and Work*, p.34. Grand Rapids Michigan: Baker Academic

[31] Bloecher, Detlef. (2004) 'Good Agency Practices: Lessons from ReMAP II'. *Connections: The Journal of the WEA Missions Commission, 3 (2),* p.12. Accessed on 13th June 2018 at: http://worldevangelicals.org/resources/rfiles/res3_124_link_1292364866.pdf

[32] Nelson, James. (2015) 'Excellence in Missions: Four Ways to Improve Field Staff Retention', *Evangelical Missions Quarterly*, Vol. 51, No. 4 pp.440-445 Accessed on 8th June 2021 at: EMQ_Volume_51_Issue_4.pdf

[33] Taylor, William D. (2002) 'Revisiting a Provocative Theme: The Attrition of Longer-Term Missionaries', *Missiology* 30 Issue 1, p.78, Accessed on 13th June 2018 at: http://journals.sagepub.com/doi/pdf/10.1177/009182960203000105

[34] See: Myers & Briggs Foundation (The). (2019) 'MBTI Basics' Florida, USA. Accessed on 21st May 2019 at: https://www.myersbriggs.org/my-mbti-personality-type/mbti-basics/home.htm?bhcp=1; DISC Personality Test (123 Test. (2019). DISC personality test. Accessed on 21st May 2019 at: https://www.123test.com/disc-personality-test/; StrengthsFinder Assessment (Gallup Inc. (2018) 'Live Your Best Life Using CliftonStrengths'. Accessed on 21st May 2019 at: https://www.gallupstrengthscenter.com/?gclid=EAIaIQobChMIlryn3O-P4gIVmwQqCh3ECACfEAAYASAAEgLY9vD_BwE; Enneagram, Your Enneagram Coach. (2019) Discover, Explore, and Become Your Best Self. Accessed on 15th July 2019 at: https://www.yourenneagramcoach.com/ and Sacred Pathways assessment by Thomas, Gary. (No date) 'Sacred Pathways - Chi Alpha Discipleship Tool' Accessed on 21st May 2019 at: https://irp-cdn.multiscreensite.com/2988a589/files/uploaded/sacred-pathways.pdf

[35] Powell, John. R. & Bowers, Joyce. M. (2002) *Enhancing Missionary Vitality*, p.112. Colorado: Mission Training International

[36] Gardener, Laura Mae. (1987) 'Proactive Care of Missionary Personnel', *Journal of Psychology & Theology* Volume 15:4, p.311. Accessed on 14th June 2018 at: http://web.b.ebscohost.com/ehost/pdfviewer/pdfviewer?vid=3&sid=f75ea4c3-f71a-464d-892c-e5a0374d5c3d%40pdc-v-sessmgr01

[37] Bosch, Brenda. (2014) *Thriving in Difficult Places: Member Care for Yourself and Others – Volume 2*, p.207. Self-Published by the author (www.thrivingmember.com) and Eenigenburg, Sue & Bliss, Robynn. (2010) *Expectations and Burnout: Women Surviving the Great Commission* p. 192-203. California: William Carey Library

[38] Van Meter, Jim. (2003) 'US Report of Findings on Missionary Retention', p.7. Accessed on 14th June 2018 at: http://www.worldevangelicals.org/resources/rfiles/res3_95_link_1292358708.pdf

[39] Shepherd, David. L. (2014) 'Promoting Missionary Mutual Care Through Spiritual Community', p.59. Accessed on 7th May 2018 at: http://digitalcommons.georgefox.edu/cgi/viewcontent.cgi?article=1085&context=dmin

[40] Bloecher, Detlef. (2005) 'Reducing Missionary Attrition (ReMAP) - what it said and what it did', p.11. Accessed on 26th May 2021 at: Microsoft Word - ReMAPI summary.doc (dmgint.de)

[41] Taylor, William D. (2002) 'Revisiting a Provocative Theme: The Attrition of Longer-Term Missionaries', p.77, *Missiology* 30 Issue 1, Accessed on 13th June 2018 at: http://journals.sagepub.com/doi/pdf/10.1177/009182960203000105

[42] Williams, D. (2010) 'Pastoral Care of Missionaries: Turning Theory into Practice', *Evangelical Missions Quarterly* Vol. 46, October 2010, No. 4, pp. 426-432

[43] Shepherd, David. L. (2014) 'Promoting Missionary Mutual Care Through Spiritual Community', p.49. Accessed on 7th May 2018 at: http://digitalcommons.georgefox.edu/cgi/viewcontent.cgi?article=1085&context=dmin

[44] Missiographics. 'Going the Distance: Missionary Retention'. (No date) Accessed on 9th April 2018 at: https://visual.ly/community/infographic/lifestyle/missionary-retention

[45] See; Wallace, Ian. (2003) *People in Aid Code of Good Practice in the Management and Support of Aid Personnel*, p.16. London: People in Aid.

[46] Hay, R. et al. (2007) *Worth Keeping: Global Perspectives on Best Practices in Missionary Retention*, p.122. Pasadena, Calif.: William Carey Library.

[47] Nelson, James. (2015) 'Excellence in Missions: Four Ways to Improve Field Staff Retention', *Evangelical Missions Quarterly*, Vol. 51, No. 4 pp.440-445 Accessed on 8th June 2021 at: EMQ_Volume_51_Issue_4.pdf

Conclusion

This book has examined factors that affect the attrition and retention of missionaries to Japan. In other words, things that cause missionaries to leave Japan and things that help them to stay. Below, I briefly summarise the conclusions in five categories: spiritual, personal, relational, practical, and agency.

In terms of spirituality, the results emphasised the centrality of God's call to missionary work in Japan. This is especially important when considering the complexities of the Japanese language and culture, the religious and spiritual barriers to Christian belief, the generally weak state of the Japanese church, and the comparatively small ministry results (see Appendix D). The survey and interview results also established the essential importance for missionaries to maintain a vibrant spiritual life in all its variety, as well as the need to be informed in the area of spiritual warfare, which is all the more important in Japan's spiritually dark atmosphere.

Regarding personal factors, the results underlined the importance of self-awareness and self-care for missionaries to Japan. Missionary self-care has been discussed for a long time, even if it hasn't always been practised. In contrast, the area of self-awareness has been less studied, for example as it pertains to gifting, approaches to relaxation, and spirituality.

In regard to human relationships, the research highlighted the needs of children, particularly their education. However, it also revealed the needs of adult children and elderly parents, raising questions of how to provide appropriate care in these areas. Furthermore, the need for community (particularly missionary community) was apparent from the results.

In the practical realm, the results established the need for language learning, both initial and ongoing, along with training in cultural understanding throughout a missionary's career. The need for sufficient finance and appropriate Bible and further training was also recognised.

As far as mission agencies are concerned, these results emphasised the need to determine 'mission or ministry fit' for new and established missionaries. It also showed the demand for competent, well-trained, empathetic leaders and supportive member care structures. The importance of 'mission or ministry fit' has long been acknowledged, but the results highlighted this importance. Likewise, interviewees particularly stressed the need to train leaders; we can't simply appoint godly, available leaders and hope they do a good job — they need training.

In conclusion, missionary retention should be regarded as a marathon rather than a sprint.[1] All missionaries to Japan and the agencies with whom they work, need to be intentional about building retention-boosting practices into their lives, ministries, and organisations. One commentator said, "Lives and fundamental values change slowly. It requires perseverance and humility of the ambassador for Christ — learning the language, understanding the culture and walking alongside the new believers, as our Jesus Christ did…his whole life, not just his last three years of ministry, changed the lives of his disciples. Likewise, it requires this long-term commitment and sacrifice that Christ will not only be Saviour but…Lord in the lives of Christians, gathered in culturally relevant, mature fellowships that are a blessing to their community and in their turn, to the nations."[2]

Finally, the primary aim of my research — and the reason why I wrote this book — is to better enable missionaries, as God's under-shepherds, to search and care for Japan's lost sheep. The biblical parable has 99 sheep in the fold and just one lost. "In Japan…it is the other way round; only one is in the fold and the other ninety-nine are still wandering astray without Christ."[3]

---

[1] Missiographics. 'Going the Distance: Missionary Retention'. (No date) Accessed on 9th April 2018 at: https://visual.ly/community/infographic/lifestyle/missionary-retention

[2] Bloecher, Detlef. (2004) 'Good Agency Practices: Lessons from ReMAP II', p.12. Connections: The Journal of the WEA Missions Commission, 3 (2), p.12-25. Accessed on 13th June 2018 at:
http://worldevangelicals.org/resources/rfiles/res3_124_link_1292364866.pdf

[3] Gosden, Eric. (1982). *The Other Ninety-Nine*, p.79. (London: Marshalls Paperbacks & The Japan Evangelistic Band)

Appendix A1:

Japan Member Care Survey

- Missionary Questionnaire

Introductory Page

Welcome to my survey as part of my final dissertation for an MA in Member Care for Redcliffe College.

Purpose of this survey:

a) To identify factors which empower missionaries to stay in Japan, as well as factors which contribute to why missionaries leave Japan.
b) This survey is *not* designed to evaluate the missionary, his/her family or the ministry they are/have been involved in.

Confidentiality & Consent:

a) The information given in this questionnaire will be handled confidentially, except in cases of harm to the individual or others. I would then be obligated to report such to supervisors or the police, as appropriate.
b) Participants may choose to remain anonymous if they desire.
c) Data collected and conclusions reached from this questionnaire (and follow-up interviews where conducted) will be written up (anonymously) and submitted as part of my Masters in Member Care. Information will also be summarised and distributed to any mission agencies or missionaries who express an interest, in order to develop administrative and member care policies which promote missionary retention.
d) Although it is not my intention, it is possible that for some respondents, completion of this survey may raise negative emotions as they reflect on their experience of mission in Japan. However, I trust that as they prayerfully reflect, they will also find God's healing.

(e) By completing and returning this questionnaire, participants give their consent for the information they supply to be used (anonymously) in this research project and distributed as stated above. Participants also accept the possibility of negative emotions being raised as they complete this survey. Participants may withdraw from the process until the results are submitted, if they wish to do so.
(f) All completed questionnaires will be deleted when the research project is completed.

Notes:

If you choose to make any comments, please ensure individuals are not identifiable.

This survey has four sections: personal details, ministering in Japan, leaving Japan (if applicable to you) and follow-up.

Thank you for participating in my survey. Your responses are important.

Section 1 – Personal Details

1) Please state your name (You may choose to remain anonymous if you prefer)

2) Please state your gender:

    ☐ Male
    ☐ Female

3) Please state your age:

    ☐ Under 30   ☐ 51-60
    ☐ 30-40   ☐ 61+
    ☐ 41-50

4) Please state your nationality:

5) Are you:

    ☐ Single   ☐ Divorced
    ☐ Married   ☐ Widowed

6) Do you have children?

    ☐ Yes
    ☐ No

7) Please state your mission agency or agencies (if applicable)

8) How many years were you, or have you been, an active missionary in Japan? (In your calculations include regular periods of furlough/home assignment in the total number of years, unless they were prolonged – i.e. more than one year)

    ☐ 0-5   ☐ 11-15   ☐ 21-25   ☐ 31-35
    ☐ 6-10   ☐ 16-20   ☐ 26-30   ☐ 36+

Section 2 – Ministering in Japan

Questions 9-14 seek to identify the factors which enabled you to stay and minister in Japan. Rate each factor from 0-5, 0 being unimportant and 5 being most relevant or important in your experience.

(For example, if a factor listed below is so important that you would have left Japan without it, rate it at 5. If, on the other hand, a factor is completely unimportant or irrelevant to you, rate it at 0.) Please rate each issue.

9) Identify the personal factors which enable(d) you to stay and minister in Japan. Rate each factor from 0-5, 0 being unimportant and 5 being most relevant or important in your experience.

- ☐ Personal devotional life
- ☐ God's call on your life to be a missionary to Japan
- ☐ Supportive marriage
- ☐ Other (Please state)

10) Identify the sending- side support factors which enable(d) you to stay and minister in Japan. Rate each factor from 0-5, 0 being unimportant and 5 being most relevant or important in your experience.

- ☐ Pastoral support (including emotional & practical) by family in your sending country
- ☐ Pastoral support (including emotional & practical) by friends in your sending country
- ☐ Pastoral support (including emotional & practical) by home or sending church(es)
- ☐ Pastoral support (including emotional & practical) by your sending side mission agency
- ☐ Financial Support
- ☐ Other (Please state)

11) Identify the pre-field training factors which enable(d) you to stay and minister in Japan. Rate each factor from 0-5, 0 being unimportant and 5 being most relevant or important in your experience.

- ☐ Practical training/internship in a church in your sending country
- ☐ Seminary/Bible training
- ☐ Life & work experience in your home country
- ☐ Your mission's pre-field orientation programme
- ☐ Other (Please state)

12) Identify the on-field training factors which enable(d) you to stay and minister in Japan. Rate each factor from 0-5, 0 being unimportant and 5 being most relevant or important in your experience.

- ☐ Your mission's on-field orientation programme
- ☐ Initial language learning provision
- ☐ Initial culture learning provision
- ☐ Ongoing language learning
- ☐ Ongoing culture learning
- ☐ Ongoing training in other relevant areas (e.g. leadership, conflict management etc.)
- ☐ Other (Please state)

13) Identify the on-field support factors (specific to your agency) which enable(d) you to stay and minister in Japan. Rate each factor from 0-5, 0 being unimportant and 5 being most relevant or important in your experience.

- ☐ Pastoral (including emotional & practical) support by family on the field
- ☐ Pastoral support (including emotional & practical) by missionary colleagues from your own agency
- ☐ Healthcare provided by your agency
- ☐ Professional advice (medical, financial, legal etc.) given by your agency
- ☐ Holiday/vacation and other allowances

- ☐ Spiritual retreats, prayer meetings or conferences etc. run by your agency
- ☐ Your mission agency's mission, vision & values
- ☐ You have been welcomed by mission leadership to be involved in developing & working towards your agency's mission, vision & values
- ☐ Other (Please state)

14) Identify the on-field support (outside your agency) which enable(d) you to stay and minister in Japan. Rate each factor from 0-5, 0 being unimportant and 5 being most relevant or important in your experience.

- ☐ Pastoral support (including emotional & practical) by missionary colleagues from other agencies
- ☐ Pastoral support (including emotional & practical) by Japanese churches, pastors and friends
- ☐ Japanese healthcare
- ☐ Availability of educational options for children
- ☐ Spiritual retreats, prayer meetings or conferences etc. run by other organisations
- ☐ Other (Please state)

15) Are you currently a missionary to Japan (either on-field or on home assignment/furlough)?

- ☐ Yes *(respondent automatically directed to Section 4)*
- ☐ No *(respondent automatically directed to Section 3)*

Section 3 – Leaving Japan

Questions 16-19 seek to identify which reasons are most relevant or important in why you left Japan. Rate each factor from 0-5, 0 being unimportant and 5 being most relevant or important in your experience.

(For example, if you left Japan largely due to children's educational issues, you might want to rate that at 5, but you may also feel, to some extent, that God was also calling you to another ministry, so might choose to rate that at 2.) Please rate each issue.

16) Identify which personal factors are most relevant or important in why you left Japan. Rate each factor from 0-5, 0 being unimportant and 5 being most relevant or important in your experience.

- ☐ God called me to another ministry
- ☐ My time in Japan was always set in a limited time-frame
- ☐ Retirement
- ☐ Sending or receiving country bureaucracy (e.g. visas, passports, permits etc.)
- ☐ Dietary or lifestyle challenges
- ☐ Physical ill-health
- ☐ Mental health issues (e.g. depression, schizophrenia, trauma post 3:11 disaster etc.)
- ☐ Fear of natural disasters (e.g. typhoons, earthquakes, volcanoes etc.)
- ☐ Stress-related issues
- ☐ Loneliness
- ☐ Bereavement
- ☐ Divorce
- ☐ Lost my Christian faith
- ☐ Lack of spiritual vitality
- ☐ Other (Please state)

17) Identify which family-related factors are most relevant or important in why you left Japan. Rate each factor from 0-5, 0 being unimportant and 5 being most relevant or important in your experience.

- ☐ My children didn't cope well with everyday life in Japan
- ☐ My children's education was not adequately provided for in Japan or elsewhere
- ☐ My adult children needed me
- ☐ My parents were ageing/unwell and needing me
- ☐ My wider family needed me
- ☐ Other (Please state)

18) Identify which ministry-related factors are most relevant or important in why you left Japan. Rate each factor from 0-5, 0 being unimportant and 5 being most relevant or important in your experience.

- ☐ Japanese language-related challenges
- ☐ Japanese culture-related challenges
- ☐ Disillusionment & discouragement about a lack of visible 'results'
- ☐ Overwork (including insufficient holiday/vacation/days off)
- ☐ Conflict within the missionary team
- ☐ Conflict with Japanese staff/team
- ☐ Individual conflict with another missionary
- ☐ Ministry 'mismatch'
- ☐ Ministry location 'mismatch'
- ☐ Spiritual attack/warfare
- ☐ Other (Please state)

19) Identify which mission agency-related factors are most relevant or important in why you left Japan. Rate each factor from 0-5, 0 being unimportant and 5 being most relevant or important in your experience.

- ☐ Retirement Policy
- ☐ Inadequate financial support
- ☐ My agency closed down
- ☐ My beliefs and/or values changed from that of my agency

- ☐ My vision and/or mission changed from that of my agency
- ☐ Marriage outside the agency and/or Japan
- ☐ No suitable post could be found for me in my agency
- ☐ Lack of 'connection' with my agency
- ☐ Conflict with my agency
- ☐ Dismissal
- ☐ Other (Please state)

Section 4 – Follow Up

20) Are you willing to take part in a follow-up interview in person or using Skype? (All interviewees are assured of confidentiality and anonymity. Records of our conversations will be destroyed when the research is complete, unless permission is expressly obtained from the interviewee.)

- ☐ Yes
- ☐ No

21) Would you like to receive a report/summary of this research's findings once it is complete?

- ☐ Yes
- ☐ No

22) If you answered 'yes' to either or both of the two previous questions, please provide your email and Skype addresses:

23) Thank you for taking time out of your busy schedule to complete this questionnaire. Please pray with me that the information gathered will serve to better care for missionaries to Japan, and that consequently, God's Kingdom work in Japan would multiply.

If you wish to make any further comments, please use the comments box below. Thank you.

Appendix A2:
Individual Missionaries Survey – Demographic Data

Q1 asked respondents to state their name if they wished to. Thirty-nine percent of respondents chose to remain anonymous, though some subsequently agreed to be interviewed.

Q2 asked respondents to state their gender. Of the 218 respondents, 117 (55.19%) were female and 95 (44.81%) were male. Six respondents skipped this question.

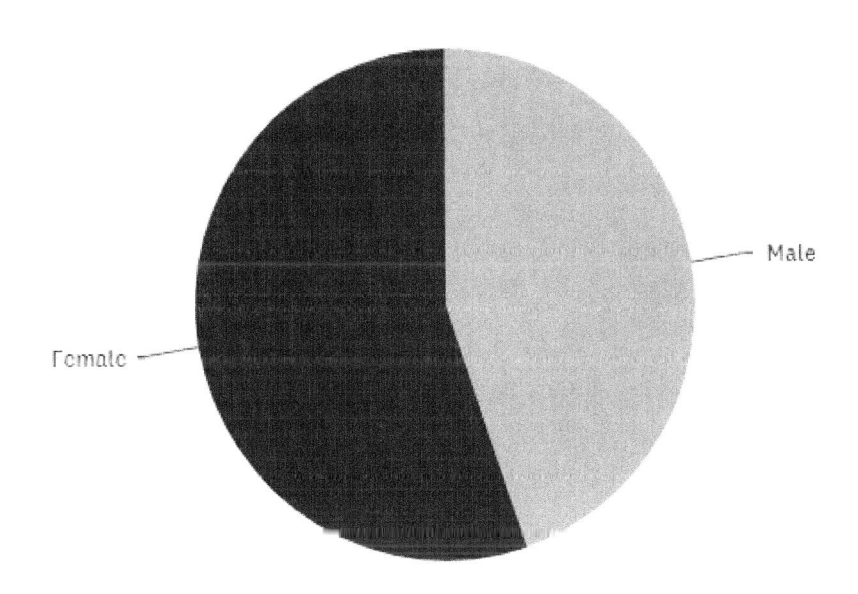

Q3 asked respondents to state their age within a range. Five respondents skipped this question.

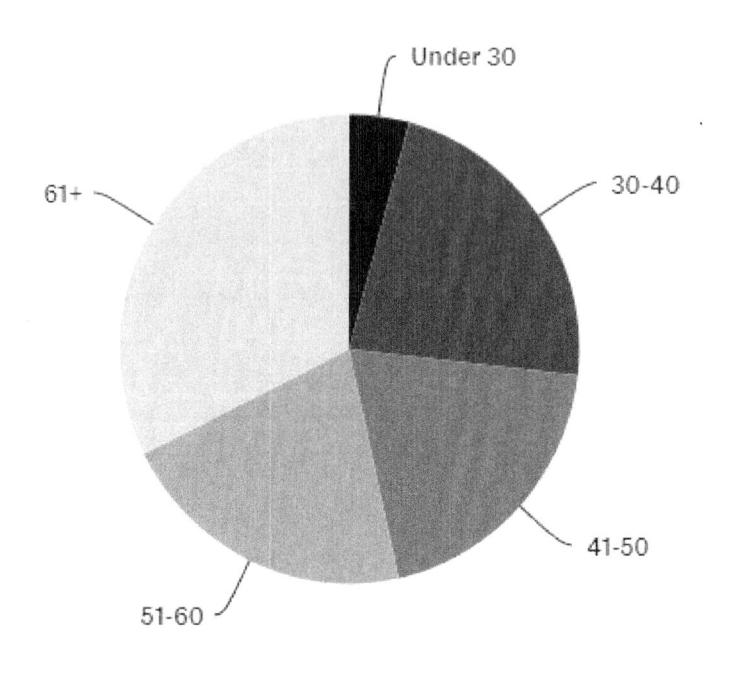

Age of survey respondents (general)

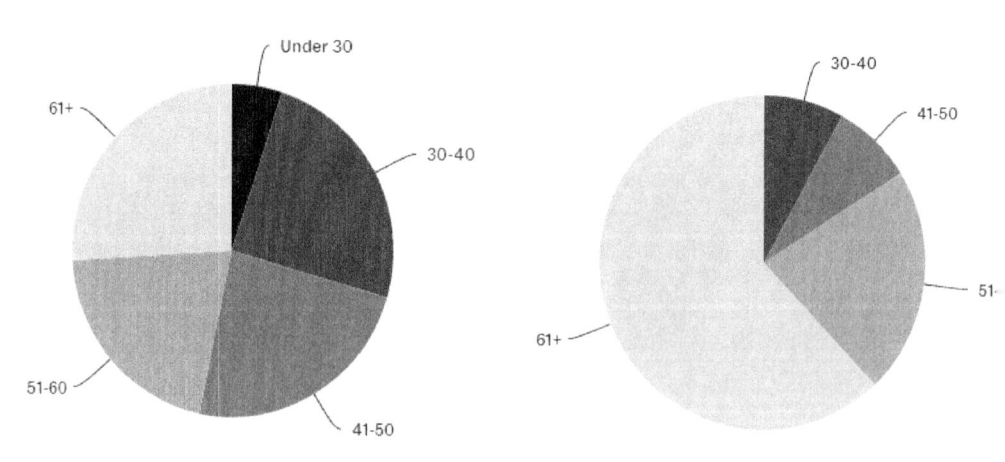

Age of current missionaries

Age of former missionaries

Q4 asked respondents to state their nationality. Eleven respondents skipped this question, and one response was spoilt.

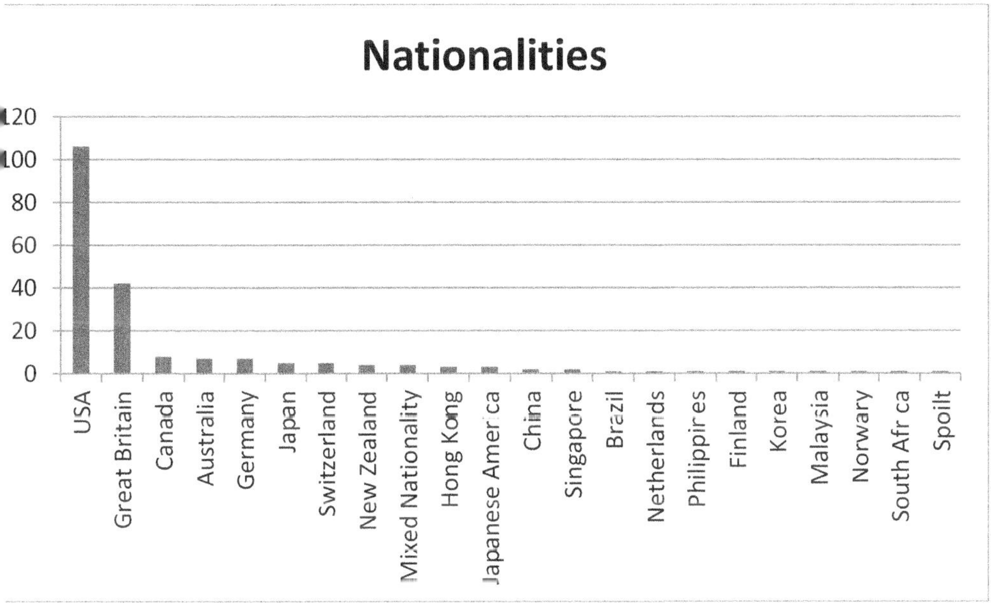
Nationalities
120
100
80
60
40
20
0
USA
Great Britain
Canada
Australia
Germany
Japan
Switzerland
New Zealand
Mixed Nationality
Hong Kong
Japanese America
China
Singapore
Brazil
Netherlands
Philippines
Finland
Korea
Malaysia
Norway
South Africa
Spoilt

Q5 asked respondents to declare their marital status. Nearly three-quarters (73.93%) of respondents were married. Seven respondents skipped this question.

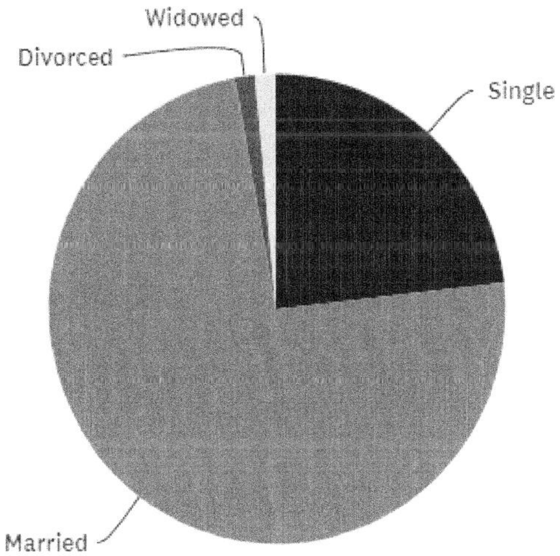
Widowed
Divorced
Single
Married

Q6 asked respondents if they had children and 66.35% said they did. Amongst married respondents, this figure rose to 87%. Seven respondents skipped this question.

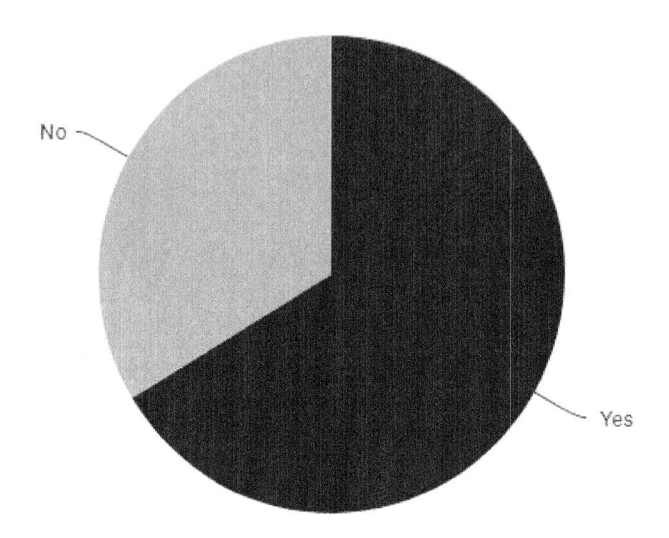

Q7 asked respondents to state their mission agency. Interestingly, 25 respondents skipped this question, perhaps out of concern of identification or in order to 'protect' their agency.

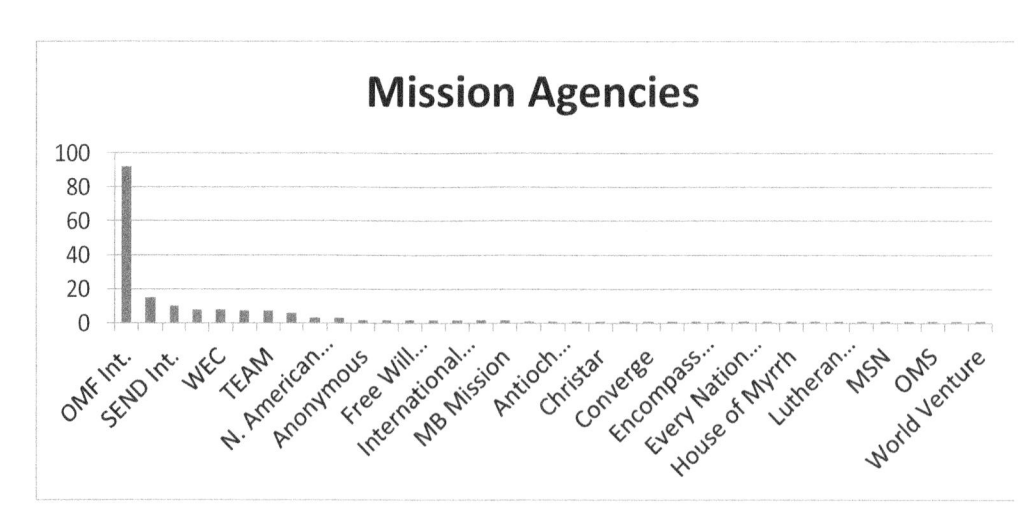

Appendix A3:

What factors led missionaries to leave Japan?

Weighted order of results from individual missionary survey

1 God's call	2.12	
2 Retirement	1.60	
3 Parents' needs	0.96	
4 Physical ill-health	0.94	
5 Ministry mismatch	0.91	
6 Stress	0.67	
6 Retirement policy	0.67	
7 Japanese language	0.60	
8 Lack of education options	0.57	
9 Overwork	0.54	
10 Adult kids' needs	0.52	
10 Japanese culture	0.52	
11 Belief and value change	0.51	
12 Mental ill-health	0.50	
13 Finance	0.49	
13 Spiritual warfare	0.49	
14 Disillusionment	0.48	
15 Conflict in missionary team	0.42	
16 Lack of spiritual vitality	0.41	
17 Loneliness	0.38	
18 Children didn't cope	0.33	
18 Conflict with individual missionaries	0.33	
19 Vision and mission change	0.30	
19 Wider family needs	0.30	
19 Ministry location mismatch	0.30	
19 Lack of agency connection	0.30	
20 Diet/lifestyle	0.27	
21 Time-limited ministry	0.25	
22 Conflict with Japanese staff	0.17	
23 No suitable post	0.13	
24 Bureaucracy	0.12	
25 Marriage outside agency	0.06	
26 Lost faith	0.04	
26 Bereavement	0.04	
26 Fear of natural disaster	0.04	
26 Divorce	0.04	
26 Dismissal	0.04	
27 Agency closed	0.00	

Appendix A4

What enables missionaries to stay in Japan?

Weighted order of results from individual missionary survey

1 God's call	4.55	
2 Devotional life	4.22	
3 Initial Language study	3.81	
4 Sending side finance	3.80	
5 Marriage	3.77	
6 Ongoing language study	3.62	
7 Missionary colleagues	3.60	
8 Ongoing culture study	3.53	
9 Seminary	3.51	
10 Experience	3.31	
11 Vision, mission, values (VMV)	3.30	
12 Holiday	3.27	
13 Sending side friends	3.15	
14 Sending side mission	3.13	
15 Japanese healthcare	3.12	
16 Japanese church	3.08	
17 Initial culture study	3.06	
18 Retreats/conferences etc.	3.04	
19 Sending side family	3.02	
20 VMV development	2.98	
21 Sending side church	2.97	
22 Ongoing training	2.92	
23 Family on field	2.75	
24 Agency healthcare	2.74	
25 Professional advice	2.69	
26 Pre-field orientation	2.60	
27 Education options	2.59	
27 Internship	2.59	
28 Retreats/conferences etc.	2.57	
29 Other missionaries	2.56	
30 On-field orientation	2.33	

Appendix B1:

Semi-structured interview questions

Thank you for allowing me to interview you, particularly in light of your experiences of care as a missionary. I reiterate that I will not use your name or details that will identify you or your organisation.

1a Share with me the highlights of why and how you came to be a missionary to Japan. What was the process of getting here for you?

1b What ministries are you or have you been involved in during your time in Japan?

2 Why and how did you choose your particular mission — or no mission?

3 What specific personal practices, or self-care, have helped/helped you stay in Japan?

Supplementary question if necessary: 3a) Give examples and explain them in more detail…

4 What specific practices (in regard to your organisation — if applicable) have helped/helped you stay in Japan?

Supplementary question if necessary: 4a) For example, mission policies, leaders, organizational structure etc.

5 What — if anything, and if applicable — would you like/have liked your mission to have done to support you more or differently in the area of member care?

Supplementary question if necessary: 5a) What suggestions do you have for mission agencies to improve organisational member care and support?

6 What advice would you give prospective and new missionaries to Japan in regard to self-care, and in choosing a mission organisation — in regard to organisational member care and support?

****

7 If you are still a missionary to Japan, what might cause you to consider leaving?

****

8 As you reflect on leaving Japan, talk me through why and how you came to that decision…

9 What — if anything — do you wish you had done differently, either in regard to self-care on the field, or in the process of leaving?

10 As you reflect on leaving Japan, how much — if at all — was your mission involved in your decision to leave (e.g. through discussion, mutual agreement, discipline, natural termination, etc.); and how — if at all — did they support you in the leaving process?

11 What — if anything — do you wish your mission had done differently?

****

12 Is there anything else you want to add about your experience in Japan as a missionary?

Appendix B2: Interviewee data

Table I: Interviewees Currently Serving in Japan

Age	Sex	Nationality	Marital status	Mission Agency	Service
61+	Female	British/New Zealand	Single	Mission Agency 1	36+
61+	Male	South African	Married	Mission Agency 2	36+
51–60	Female	American	Married	Independent	31–35
51–60	Male	American	Married	Mission Agency 3	26–30
51–60	Female	British	Married	Mission Agency 4	16–20
30–40	Male	American	Married	Mission Agency 5	11–15
41–50	Female	Australian	Single	Mission Agency 6	6–10
30–40	Male	Hong Kong	Married	Mission Agency 2	0–5

Table II: Interviewees No Longer Serving in Japan

Age	Sex	Nationality	Marital status	Mission Agency	Service
61+	Male	British	Married	Mission Agency 2	26–30
51–60	Female	German	Married	Mission Agency 1	21–25
51–60	Female	American	Married	Mission Agency 2	21–25
51–60	Male	American	Married	Mission Agency 7	21–25
41–50	Female	New Zealand	Single	Mission Agency 2	16–20
51–60	Female	American	Married	Mission Agency 8	6–10
30–40	Male	British	Married	Mission Agency 2	0–5

Appendix C: Research methodology

This appendix explains my research methods, including my chosen research methods of questionnaires and semi-structured interviews, data collection and analysis, and ethical issues arising from the research.

Research methods

Both qualitative and quantitative approaches were helpful for examining the retention and attrition of missionaries to Japan.

Qualitative research "counts and describes 'what is out there.'"[1] providing numerical data.[2] For this aspect of research, I used an online survey (Survey Monkey), which enabled me to quickly gain data from many participants worldwide, analyse it easily, identify trends and draw valid generalisations.[3] However, the survey was inevitably limited in reach and produced brief, potentially incomplete answers. It thus needed to be supplemented by qualitative research.

Qualitative research provides descriptive textual information.[4] Therefore, I conducted semi-structured interviews to understand participants' insights and experience, including previously unconsidered issues. Since these interviews were labour-intensive, risked interviewer/interviewee bias, and gathered a lot of information, I used QDA Miner Lite for coding and analysis.

In summary, I used online surveys and semi-structured interviews to collect and analyse data and used grounded theory[5] to examine emerging themes and gain insights into retention, attrition, agency member care, and self-care.

The research project

I now consider the research project in detail including rationale, process, strengths and weaknesses of the methods, and ethical issues.

Desk research

I chose to examine attrition *and* retention because knowing why missionaries leave Japan is important, but knowing what helps them stay more important still. Therefore, I studied books, articles, and websites about member care, largely related to missionaries, but also aid workers. This literature review (not included in this book) provided background to my field research and enabled me to examine related issues thoroughly.

Field research: Online survey

Fieldwork was essential, because, to the best of my knowledge, no previous studies of missionary retention and attrition in Japan had been done. Therefore, I conducted two anonymous (to prevent cautious responses) online survey/questionnaires amongst current and former missionaries and amongst mission/personnel leaders (not included in this book). For consistency, both surveys were similar in content.[6] I wanted to compare the experience and opinions of missionaries with those of mission leaders, to see where they agreed and how they differed.[7]

The surveys offered six options for each factor, from zero (unimportant) to five (most relevant/important). However, on reflection, it would have been helpful to also include the option of "Not applicable".

Missionaries' survey

Identical questionnaires (Appendix A1) were sent to current and former missionaries. They were carefully worded to counteract possible sensitivity about having left Japan. They simply asked respondents to identify factors that helped them to stay in Japan and factors that affected their departure, where appropriate. The survey included questions about personal data, because I felt that it might be valuable to know whether marital status, sex, age or nationality affected certain factors. However, some respondents chose not to answer these questions. The questionnaire was tested before distribution, to check understanding and ease of completion. To simplify participation, current missionaries were able to skip questions concerning leaving and were automatically directed to questions regarding interview participation.

The survey was quick to send to those on the Japan Evangelical Missionary Association (JEMA) mailing list and to former missionaries known to me. It took about 10 minutes to complete, leading to a relatively high response and completion rate. Of the approximately 1070 recipients, 218 people (20%) responded. However, participants were unable to provide explanations for their answers (apart from a few comments), meaning the collected data was limited and incomplete. Also, because the survey was not personally administered, people might misunderstand the questions[8] and provide potentially flawed data. In addition, some respondents did not complete the survey and others struggled to use the software. Finally, some people dislike online surveys and may have chosen not to participate, while others may have forgotten to do so.

I endeavoured to counteract these issues by explaining myself, the research, and how to complete the survey. On reflection, I should have suggested participants read the entire survey first, as several commented on factors mentioned in subsequent questions, leading to repetition and perhaps frustration for participants and unnecessarily full 'comments' boxes.

Mission/Personnel Leaders' Survey

After analysing the data from both surveys, it became clear that I had too much data to include the mission/personnel leaders' survey in my dissertation. Therefore, this information is not included in this book and no comments are offered.

Online survey: Data analysis

Although expensive, Survey Monkey was largely easy to use and provided useful analysis and helpful graphics.

Field research: Semi-structured interviews

Although the survey information was valuable, it was brief and rather impersonal, so the interviews were designed to 'make it real'. Initial questions aimed to help interviewees relax, so these results are not presented in the dissertation nor in this book. I used open questions, allowing interviewees to answer as they thought best[9] (Appendix B1).

The purpose of the interviews was to gain a general picture of factors related to missionary retention and attrition and to examine any variations revealed by differences. I used stratified sampling to identify interviewees[10], including men and women; singles, marrieds, and those with families; different ages, differing lengths of service, different nationalities and agency affiliation, where applicable. I interviewed one Asian missionary, who might offer a different perspective[11] and missionaries serving in rural and urban areas, throughout Japan. To reflect survey respondents and missionaries in Japan, I interviewed eight current missionaries, seven former missionaries, six Americans, six missionaries from the largest agency in Japan, 12 married and three single missionaries, ranging from 30–61+ in age and 0–36+ years of service, representing eight mission agencies (Appendix B2).

I conducted pilot interviews, enabling me to simplify questions and give examples. All interviewees were given a participation information sheet and completed a consent form (not included in this book). Interviewees were assured of confidentiality and anonymity and that records would be destroyed when the research was complete.

I interviewed everyone by video call, saving time and money and providing a neutral environment[12], avoiding bias resulting from different interview conditions. I also sought to reduce bias by helping interviewees relax, sticking closely to the questions, and allowing adequate response time, without undue interruption. Following pilot interviewees' suggestions, I sent the questions beforehand, suggesting interviewees think through their responses, without actually preparing answers. However, I recognise that not all interviewees may have done so, possibly leading to disparity. Nonetheless, without seeing questions beforehand, some interviewees might have been unable to answer as fully or quickly. This pre-interview email clarified the approximate interview length, fulfilling another pilot interviewee's suggestion of providing broad guidance about expected detail.

Participants were interviewed over a period of three months, within five months of completing the survey. Skype was essential, but weak internet connections and diverse time zones were challenging. I tried to conduct interviews at the most convenient time for interviewees.[13] I used Otter (https://otter.ai/) to transcribe the interviews, which helped me concentrate on the speaker and allowed faster transcription. However, Otter's accuracy varies with different accents and became more inaccurate as interviewees relaxed. All transcripts were checked and agreed by interviewees before analysis.

These interviews allowed me to gather personal responses, to clarify meaning when required, and to ask follow-up questions where appropriate. However, they were time consuming to complete and analyse and were inevitably influenced by me as the interviewer, despite attempts to reduce bias.[14]

Semi-structured interviews: Data analysis

The interviews generated a lot of data, so coding was essential for analysis.[15] Using QDA Miner Lite, I began with line-by-line coding[16] to identify key words in each transcript, followed by focused or selective coding[17] to group emerging themes together. The software analysed large amounts of text and identified themes easily, displaying how often and in how many interviews themes occurred, as well as producing helpful graphs. This analysis corroborated issues raised by the literature review and survey, as well as raising one additional topic.

Ethical issues

"Ethical issues permeate interview research"[18] as the interviewer attempts to balance the pursuit of knowledge with respect for the interviewee.

To ensure confidentiality, I used private email and survey accounts, obtained the informed consent of participants, along with their permission to use collected data anonymously. Participants were guaranteed anonymity (except in cases of actual or anticipated harm to self or others) and could withdraw at any time. All information was stored securely and destroyed after the research was completed.

To reduce bias, I interviewed a variety of missionaries, including those I knew personally and those I had never met before and those with different roles. Regarding reducing power imbalance, unintended assumptions, and flawed conclusions, I aimed to build trust with survey respondents and interviewees by ensuring confidentiality, using questions to put interviewees at ease, asking open questions, and allowing interviewees to respond freely without unnecessary comment.[19] I also strove to maintain objectivity and honesty in the presentation and analysis of data collected.[20]

Finally, because the subject of this research may provoke negative emotions, participants were informed of this beforehand and I prepared a list of resources for anyone who expressed a desire for support, though none requested additional help. Encouragingly, some participants expressed thanks for care received, what they had learnt, and how God had used them, even through negative experiences.

---

[1] Sapsford, Roger. (2006) *Survey Research*, p.1. 2nd revised edition. Los Angeles/London/New Delhi/Singapore/Washington DC: SAGE Publications Ltd.
[2] McMillan, Kathleen and Weyers, Jonathan. (2008) *How to Write Dissertations & Project Reports*, p.109. England: Pearson Education Limited.
[3] Cottrell, Stella. (2014) *Dissertations and Project Reports: A step by step guide*, p.93. UK/USA: Palgrave Macmillan.
[4] McMillan, Kathleen and Weyers, Jonathan. (2008) *How to Write Dissertations & Project Reports*, p.123. England: Pearson Education Limited.
[5] Charmaz, Kathy. (2004) 'Grounded Theory', *The SAGE Encyclopedia of Social Science Research Methods*, p.2, Sage Research Methods, Sage Publications Inc.
[6] Sapsford, Roger. (2006) *Survey Research*, p.5. 2nd revised edition. Los Angeles/London/New Delhi/Singapore/Washington DC: SAGE Publications Ltd.
[7] Ibid, p.8
[8] Seale, Clive. (1998) *Researching Society & Culture*, p.127. Los Angeles/London/New Delhi/Singapore/Washington DC: Sage Publications Ltd.
[9] Sarantakos, Sotirios. (1998) *Social Research*, p.179. 2nd revised edition. UK/USA: Palgrave Macmillan.
[10] Seale, Clive. (1998) *Researching Society & Culture*, p.137. Los Angeles/London/New Delhi/Singapore/Washington DC: Sage Publications Ltd.
[11] Disproportionate Stratification – Seale, Clive. (1998) *Researching Society & Culture*, p.137. Los Angeles/London/New Delhi/Singapore/Washington DC: Sage Publications Ltd.
[12] Sarantakos, Sotirios. (1998) *Social Research*, p.182. 2nd revised edition. UK/USA: Palgrave Macmillan.
[13] Ibid, p.192
[14] Ibid, p.199
[15] Seale, Clive. (1998) *Researching Society & Culture*, p.130. Los Angeles/London/New Delhi/Singapore/Washington DC: Sage Publications Ltd.
[16] Charmaz, Kathy. (2004) 'Grounded Theory', *The SAGE Encyclopedia of Social Science Research Methods*, p.5, Sage Research Methods, Sage Publications Inc.
[17] Ibid, p.6

[18] Kvale, Steinar and Brinkmann Svend. (2009) *InterViews: Learning the Craft of Qualitative Research Interviewing*, p.16. 2nd edition. Los Angeles/London/New Delhi/Singapore/Washington DC: Sage Publications Inc.
[19] Creswell John W. (2013) *Qualitative Inquiry & Research Design: Choosing Among Five Approaches*, p.60. 3rd revised edition. Los Angeles/London/New Delhi/Singapore/Washington DC: SAGE Publications, Inc.
[20] Ibid, p.66

Appendix D: Japanese context

An understanding of the Japanese context and its impact on missionaries is valuable as we consider the hazards and health of missionaries to Japan.

Japanese history

To understand modern Japan in all its complexity and breadth, an appreciation of its history is vital. The present is rooted in the past and that history heavily influences Japan's present-day culture.[1]

Japan was settled from about 8000 BC[2], but from the eighth century AD onwards there have been few large influxes of people.[3] This high level of homogeneity unites Japanese people, but it can be challenging for foreign missionaries, who are not part of this unified culture. Japan's earliest written historical records are replete with creation myths, gods (including a presumed ancestor of Japan's Emperor), and goddesses[4], and these provide the foundation of Shintoism.[5]

Chinese writing was adopted in Japan during the period AD 250–646[6] and later Prince Shōtoku (AD 574-622) established Buddhism[7], while maintaining Shintoism at the same time. Shōtoku likened the religious landscape of Japan to a tree: Shinto is the roots, lying at the heart of the Japanese psyche; Confucianism is the trunk and branches, influencing politics, morality, and education; and Buddhism is the flowering of religious feelings.[8] This highly syncretistic worldview continues to profoundly affect evangelism and Christianity in Japan.

Medieval Japan saw Zen Buddhism develop as the samurai's creed.[9] Feudal lords Oda Nobunaga (1534–1582), Toyotomi Hideyoshi (1537–1598) and Tokugawa Ieyasu (1543–1616) followed, styling themselves as gods and unifying Japan.[10] During the period 1603–1868, rigid Confucian-based societal distinctions developed,[11] and these influences continue to shape Japan and Japanese Christianity.

During the 1800s, Japan became increasingly imperialistic.[12] The Meiji Restoration (1868) and Meiji Constitution (1889) saw power returned to the imperial court, fuelling industrialisation, modernisation, and nationalism.[13] The government sought to unite people through Shintoism[14], which affected, and still affects, how Japanese Christians and Christianity are perceived. Japan's militaristic stance[15] led to their alliance with Germany[16], the atomic bombings, Japan's defeat and ruination, and American occupation.[17] These events continue to significantly affect the psyche of Japanese people today. Japan is a proud, independent island nation, which is vehemently anti-war.

Japan rebuilt itself after World War II, becoming a leader in many fields[18], yet the bubble of prosperity burst in 1991.[19] The Tokyo sarin gas attack in 1995[20] generated unease and suspicion about religion in general and Christian evangelisation in particular. The earthquake, tsunami, and nuclear meltdown in 2011 killed about 20,000 people and affected many more.[21] This cataclysmic event led to fresh evangelism partnerships, although they haven't as yet seen much fruit. The speed and degree of change in Japan since the beginning of the Heisei era in 1989 has been astonishing.[22]

Japanese culture and language

"Every country is different…but Japan is more different than any other."[23] Another author says you have to be born into 'Japaneseness', "…steeped…in it at a genetic level."[24]

Japanese culture developed in relative isolation. Because of Japan's mountainous landscape, people were thrown together, creating cultural characteristics like the desire for harmony, group consciousness, and implicit and ambiguous communication.[25] Gosden commented, "Japan was isolated. The result? An ingrown culture, self-sufficient…asking nothing of others and seeking no approval from others…a strong obstinacy to change, and a fear…and…rejection of outside influence."[26] De Mente commented on *nihonjinron* (the theory of Japanese uniqueness), mentioning the "obvious" division between Japan and the rest of the world, and the innate correctness of "the Japanese way".[27] These distinctives can make penetrating Japanese culture challenging, in terms of friendship and Christian ministry.

Furthermore, Japanese culture is multi-layered being made up of Shintoism, Buddhism, Taoism, Confucianism, and modern Western influences.[28] Benedict noted that Japanese culture was not purely Buddhism nor Confucianism, but uniquely Japanese.[29] Shintoism is animistic, with no explicit moral code or concept of sin.[30] Worshippers seek blessing and protection from many gods[31] and revere nature, but they lack the concept of a Creator. This makes it challenging to teach about the one Creator God, who loves sinners.

Japanese Buddhism emphasises freedom from pain and rewards for good deeds.[32] It includes Zen Buddhist values such as obligation, sacrifice, and perseverance.[33] These values can both positively and negatively influence Christian ministry. For example, some Japanese may accept the Christian message merely out of obligation; on the other hand, many Japanese Christians show remarkable sacrifice and perseverance for the sake of Christ. Missionaries, seeking to adapt to the culture, can sacrifice too much and serve beyond healthy levels. Japanese Buddhism, influenced by Confucianism[34], also embraces ancestor worship.[35] Many

Japanese struggle to become Christians because they don't want to be cursed by their ancestors[36] or be separated from family by going to heaven.[37]

Confucianism promotes a harmonious, ritualistic, and hierarchical society[38] expressed through traits like filial piety and status-related forms of address and bowing.[39] This leads to conformity, group-consciousness,[40] and social harmony (*wa*). Doi noted how incredibly hard it is for Japanese to act independently of the group.[41] How difficult, therefore, to become a Christian and disrupt the *wa*. Moreover, this concept can cause wariness towards outsiders like missionaries, because as De Mente noted, they cannot fit in to Japan simply because they are not Japanese.[42] Nakane called this "the complete estrangement of people 'outside' our world."[43] These concepts can hinder evangelism and discipleship and may negatively impact the longevity of missionaries due to a possible lack of acceptance and deep relationships, as well as slow progress in ministry.

Furthermore, not only are Shintoism, Buddhism, and Confucianism all present in Japan, Japanese people commonly follow more than one religion.[44] However, this syncretism is mixed with a subtle altering of beliefs and practices to suit the Japanese context[45], which is sometimes called "Japanization".[46] These elements affect evangelism — and especially discipleship — as missionaries preach the exclusive and uncompromising claims of Christ.

The Japanese language reflects this multifaceted and complex culture, consisting of two syllabaries and thousands of pictograms, all used concurrently. Japan's first missionary, Francis Xavier, called Japanese "the devil's own tongue"[47]; many missionaries may sympathise. Furthermore, some words, such as sin, righteousness, and redemption, have different nuances in Japanese compared to their equivalents in English translations of the Bible.[48] The Japanese language is a substantial barrier, and some missionaries struggle to overcome it throughout their missionary service in Japan.

Missionaries need to understand and adapt appropriately to Japanese culture and to employ the Japanese language competently and attractively to explain the gospel. Done well, this challenging undertaking brings great joy for the missionary to Japan, but language difficulties and culture shock can cause stress and disillusionment and it may seem like Christianity will never penetrate.

Japanese mission and church history

Christianity in Japan can be broadly divided into three main eras.[49]

1549–1859

Most sources agree that Francis Xavier and the Jesuits introduced Christianity to Japan in 1549[50], with about 300,000 converts by 1600.[51] Despite sporadic persecution, people were largely free to practise Christianity. However, Toyotomi Hideyoshi, fearful of the church's influence, banned missionaries in 1587[52], leading to the crucifixion of 26 martyrs (1597).[53] Tokugawa Ieyasu also banned Christianity and expelled missionaries in 1614[54], with at least 4,000 Christians martyred and many more horrifically persecuted between 1614–1640.[55] A crisis point arrived in 1637, and Japan closed its borders in 1639 for over 200 years.[56]

1859–1945

Japan reopened in 1854[57] and missionaries poured in during subsequent years, but were distrusted and restricted[58] and their hearers were antagonistic.[59] After reopening, some 'hidden Christians' emerged[60] with many declaring their faith publicly, leading to torture and exile. The ban on Christianity was lifted in 1873, because of Japan's desire for trade and recognition by the West, although there was no internal change of heart.[61] Threatened by Christianity, state Shinto evolved during the Meiji Restoration, leading to Christians being severely persecuted.[62] Fujiwara states, "Shinto…reigned over all religions in Japan…; In its first encounter with Christianity, Japan adopted an isolationist policy to block out Christianity; in its second encounter…it created state Shinto."[63]

In the early 1900s, evangelism began through local and denominational campaigns[64]; Christian schools were started and some revival broke out, with Christians involved in social welfare after the Great Kanto Earthquake (1923). However, from 1933–1934, the Catholic church was persecuted, with churches destroyed and missionaries expelled.[65] Subsequently, some churches compromised with Japanese nationalism[66] and Protestant churches were ordered to unite in 1941.[67] "The 'People's Rite' was…compulsory in…church services…bowing …turning towards the Imperial Palace, singing the national anthem and reading some imperial rescript."[68] Those who refused to compromise were persecuted.[69]

1945–Present

After the war, full religious freedom was granted, Shinto was separated from the State and the Emperor's divinity renounced.[70] However, religious freedom was "not something created by the Japanese…it was imposed by the occupying forces."[71] Many Christians repented of nationalistic compromise and the church was re-established.[72] About 3,000 American missionaries entered Japan, Christianity boomed and Christian schools and universities were established. Trevor commented "The effect of defeat and invasion…coupled with the denial of their national faith…was shattering, leading many to search for another focus for their personal and national lives."[73]

However, as Japan regained its sovereignty (1951–1952) and the economy began to boom, people looked less to religion.[74] More missionaries and agencies began working in Japan during the 1950s, holding mass evangelistic campaigns. However, Japanese communism and the issues of world peace, nuclear disarmament, and economic prosperity led many to leave the church in the 1970s.[75] The 1980s saw some evangelistic campaigns (despite waning popularity) and children's Sunday school attendance began falling; though in the 1990s, the charismatic movement saw some conversions.[76]

Christianity in Japan has flourished, been persecuted, compromised and ignored. However, "for its relatively small size, the influence of Christianity in Japanese society has been extraordinary."[77] Nevertheless, Japan's mission and church history could leave missionaries feeling dispirited and despondent. Some may agree with the apostate priest in Shusaku Endo's novel *Silence*, who reflects that neither banning Christianity nor the persecution of Christians have been the death of Christianity in Japan; there's something about Japan that smothers Christianity.[78]

The church in Japan

"'There is no country in the world where the church has sown the gospel so generously, yet reaped so sparingly.'"[79] Despite accessibility and a long missionary history, the Japanese are the world's second largest unreached people group[80], with only 0.84% Christian.[81]

The church's annual growth rate is —0.2% (i.e., it is shrinking) and attracting new members is like "trying 'to draw water with a bamboo basket'"[82]. Many places are without a church or adequate witness. Mehn calculated that Japan needs 50,000 to 120,000 churches.[83] This discouraging situation and monumental task can cause missionaries to feel overwhelmed, questioning whether they are making any difference.

Examining the Japanese church's characteristics, the culture of assimilation can blur the line between appropriate enculturation and syncretism[84], leading to possible compromise and dilution of the gospel.[85] Moreover, the general cultural acceptance of the status quo means churches can find innovation challenging and many of them stick to time-honoured models. Balancing enculturation and syncretism, innovation and tradition, is tough in this context.

Japan's Confucian-based hierarchical structure profoundly affects the church, leading to clergy-centric leadership[86], teaching by the pastor alone,[87] and a weakened understanding of the priesthood of all believers (1 Peter 2:9), resulting in fewer confident gospel witnesses.[88] This is exceptionally challenging for missionaries seeking to equip Japanese believers to evangelise and lead.

Mehn and others note that many churches are insular and do not engage their community[89] This perhaps stems from Japan's isolationist history, the culture of not wanting to bother anyone, insufficient numbers or resources, an inferiority complex, or a fortress mentality. Lee commented, "the Church must run from its insular, bunker mentality to engage with society."[90] Missionaries too battle against this insularity.

Lewis and others have commented on spiritual resistance in Japan.[91] Mehn noted that "the main hindrance…in Japan is not just conceptual, cultural, or practical but ultimately spiritual."[92] Though largely unquantifiable, the effects of spiritual warfare in Japan must not be underestimated.

The Japanese church has a high proportion of women and is largely well-educated and middle class.[93] Gosden notes the difficulty of reaching the upper and working classes[94]. Urging family and community outreach, a Bible college principal said the, "slow nature of church growth…indicates the individualistic pattern" of evangelism.[95] However, family outreach is difficult due to long working hours, insufficient family time[96], and children whose lives are bursting with activities.

Mehn concluded, "the Japanese are the epitome of a people unresponsive to the gospel. Japan presents…formidable cultural, historical, sociological, and spiritual challenges for evangelism."[97] Like the priest in Shusaku Endo's novel *Silence*, Japan's demanding context could leave missionaries feeling defeated by missionary work.[98]

---

[1] Davies, Roger J. (2016) *Japanese Culture: The Religious and Philosophical Foundations*, p.25-26. (USA, Singapore & Japan: Tuttle Publishing)
[2] Mason, R.H.P. & Caiger, J.G. (1997) *A History of Japan. Revised Edition*, p.19. Japan, USA & Singapore: Tuttle Publishing
[3] Davies, Roger J. (2016) *Japanese Culture: The Religious and Philosophical Foundations*, p.16. USA, Singapore & Japan: Tuttle Publishing
[4] Lee, Samuel C. (2011) *Understanding Japan: Through the eyes of Christian faith. Fourth Edition*, p.5. Amsterdam: Foundation University Press
[5] Clements, Jonathan. (2017) *A Brief History of Japan: Samurai, Shogun and Zen: The Extraordinary Story of the Land of the Rising Sun*, p.34. USA, Singapore & Japan: Tuttle Publishing
[6] Davies, Roger J. (2016) *Japanese Culture: The Religious and Philosophical Foundations*, p.18-19. USA, Singapore & Japan: Tuttle Publishing
[7] Clements, Jonathan. (2017) *A Brief History of Japan: Samurai, Shogun and Zen: The Extraordinary Story of the Land of the Rising Sun,* p.71. USA, Singapore & Japan: Tuttle Publishing
[8] Davies, Roger J. (2016) *Japanese Culture: The Religious and Philosophical Foundations*, p.39. USA, Singapore & Japan: Tuttle Publishing
[9] Clements, Jonathan. (2017) *A Brief History of Japan: Samurai, Shogun and Zen: The Extraordinary Story of the Land of the Rising Sun*, p.108. USA, Singapore & Japan: Tuttle Publishing
[10] Ibid, p.140-143.

[11] Lee, Samuel C. (2011) *Understanding Japan: Through the eyes of Christian faith. Fourth Edition*, p.17. Amsterdam: Foundation University Press

[12] Clements, Jonathan. (2017) *A Brief History of Japan: Samurai, Shogun and Zen: The Extraordinary Story of the Land of the Rising Sun*, p.199-200. USA, Singapore & Japan: Tuttle Publishing

[13] Fujiwara, Atsuyoshi. (2012) *Theology of Culture in a Japanese Context*, p.211. Oregon: Pickwick Publications

[14] Ibid, p.212.

[15] Clements, Jonathan. (2017) *A Brief History of Japan: Samurai, Shogun and Zen: The Extraordinary Story of the Land of the Rising Sun*, p.211. USA, Singapore & Japan: Tuttle Publishing

[16] Mason, R.H.P. & Caiger, J.G. (1997) *A History of Japan. Revised Edition*, p.343. Japan, USA & Singapore: Tuttle Publishing

[17] Lee, Samuel C. (2011) *Understanding Japan: Through the eyes of Christian faith. Fourth Edition*, p.23. Amsterdam: Foundation University Press

[18] Ibid p.23.

[19] Clements, Jonathan. (2017) *A Brief History of Japan: Samurai, Shogun and Zen: The Extraordinary Story of the Land of the Rising Sun*, p.252. USA, Singapore & Japan: Tuttle Publishing

[20] BBC News. (2018) 'Aum Shinrikyo: Images from the 1995 Tokyo Sarin attack'. Accessed on 2nd July 2019 at: https://www.bbc.com/news/in-pictures-43629706

[21] Kingston, Jeff. (2013) *Contemporary Japan: History, Politics & Social Change Since the 1980s*, p.20. UK: John Wiley & Sons Ltd

[22] Ibid, p.20.

[23] Doughill, John. (2016) *In Search of Japan's Hidden Christians*, p.17. UK: SPCK

[24] Clements, Jonathan. (2017) *A Brief History of Japan: Samurai, Shogun and Zen: The Extraordinary Story of the Land of the Rising Sun*, p.136. USA, Singapore & Japan: Tuttle Publishing

[25] Davies, Roger J. & Ikeno, Osamu. (2002) *The Japanese Mind: Understanding Contemporary Japanese Culture*, p.10-11. USA, Singapore & Japan: Tuttle Publishing.

[26] Gosden, Eric. (1982). *The Other Ninety-Nine*, p.20. London: Marshalls Paperbacks & The Japan Evangelistic Band

[27] De Mente, Boyé Lafayette. (2003) *Kata: The Key to Understanding & Dealing with the Japanese*, p.2. USA and Japan: Tuttle Publishing

[28] Davies, Roger J. (2016) *Japanese Culture: The Religious and Philosophical Foundations*, p.31-2. USA, Singapore & Japan: Tuttle Publishing

[29] Benedict, Ruth. (1946) *The Chrysanthemum and the Sword*, p.19. USA & Japan: Tuttle Publishing (2000)

[30] Lee, Samuel C. (2011) *Understanding Japan: Through the eyes of Christian faith. Fourth Edition*, p.92. Amsterdam: Foundation University Press

[31] Gosden, Eric. (1982). *The Other Ninety-Nine*, p.41. London: Marshalls Paperbacks & The Japan Evangelistic Band

[32] Ayabe, Henry. (1992) *Step Inside*, p.122. Tokyo: Japan Evangelical Missionary Association

[33] De Mente, Boyé Lafayette. (2004) *The Japanese Samurai Code*, p.9. USA and Japan: Tuttle Publishing
[34] Cortazzi, Hugh. (1994) *Modern Japan: A Concise Survey*, p.8. Japan: The Japan Times
[35] Davies, Roger J. (2016) *Japanese Culture: The Religious and Philosophical Foundations*, p.36. USA, Singapore & Japan: Tuttle Publishing
[36] Davies, Roger J. & Ikeno, Osamu. (2002) *The Japanese Mind: Understanding Contemporary Japanese Culture*, p.120. USA, Singapore & Japan: Tuttle Publishing
[37] Lee, Samuel C. (2011) *Understanding Japan: Through the eyes of Christian faith. Fourth Edition*, p.95. Amsterdam: Foundation University Press
[38] Cortazzi, Hugh. (1994) *Modern Japan: A Concise Survey*, p.7. Japan: The Japan Times
[39] Benedict, Ruth. (1946) *The Chrysanthemum and the Sword*, p.47-51. USA & Japan: Tuttle Publishing (2000)
[40] De Mente, Boyé Lafayette. (2008) *Etiquette Guide to Japan*, p.16. (USA and Japan: Tuttle Publishing)
[41] Doi, Takeo. (1973) *The Anatomy of Dependence*, p.54. (USA: Kodansha America)
[42] De Mente, Boyé Lafayette. (2003) *Kata: The Key to Understanding & Dealing with the Japanese*, p.13. USA and Japan: Tuttle Publishing
[43] Nakane, Chie. (1970) *Japanese Society*, p.21. California: University of California
[44] Davies, Roger J. (2016) *Japanese Culture: The Religious and Philosophical Foundations*, p.33. USA, Singapore & Japan: Tuttle Publishing
[45] Ibid, p.37
[46] Lee, Samuel C. (2011) *Understanding Japan: Through the eyes of Christian faith. Fourth Edition*, p.21. Amsterdam: Foundation University Press
[47] Doughill, John. (2016) *In Search of Japan's Hidden Christians*, p.24. UK: SPCK
[48] Ayabe, Henry. (1992) *Step Inside*, p.119-140. Tokyo: Japan Evangelical Missionary Association
[49] Fujiwara, Atsuyoshi. (2012) *Theology of Culture in a Japanese Context*, p.182. Oregon: Pickwick Publications
[50] Lewis, David. C. (1993) *The Unseen Face of Japan*, p.247. UK: Monarch
[51] Doughill, John. (2016) *In Search of Japan's Hidden Christians*, p. xi. UK: SPCK
[52] Gosden, Eric. (1982). *The Other Ninety-Nine*, p.17. London: Marshalls Paperbacks & The Japan Evangelistic Band
[53] Taylor, William D., Van Der Meer, Antonia, Reimer Reg. (2012) *Sorrow & Blood: Christian Mission in Contexts of Suffering, Persecution, and Martyrdom*, p.188. (Globalization of Mission). Pasadena: William Carey Library
[54] Endo, Shusaku. (Translated by William Johnston) (1969) *Silence*, p. xi. USA: Picador Modern Classics (2016)
[55] Doughill, John. (2016) *In Search of Japan's Hidden Christians*, p. xi. UK: SPCK
[56] Taylor, William D., Van Der Meer, Antonia, Reimer Reg. (2012) *Sorrow & Blood: Christian Mission in Contexts of Suffering, Persecution, and Martyrdom*, p.189. (Globalization of Mission). Pasadena: William Carey Library
[57] Fujiwara, Atsuyoshi. (2012) *Theology of Culture in a Japanese Context*, p.210. Oregon: Pickwick Publications

[58] Trevor, Hugh. (Undated) *Japan's Post-War Protestant Churches*, p.10. Unpublished – kept by OMF Japan
[59] Fujiwara, Atsuyoshi. (2012) *Theology of Culture in a Japanese Context*, p.211. Oregon: Pickwick Publications
[60] Doughill, John. (2016) *In Search of Japan's Hidden Christians*, p. xii. UK: SPCK
[61] Lee, Samuel C. (2011) *Understanding Japan: Through the eyes of Christian faith. Fourth Edition*, p.85. Amsterdam: Foundation University Press
[62] Fujiwara, Atsuyoshi. (2012) *Theology of Culture in a Japanese Context*, p.228. Oregon: Pickwick Publications
[63] Ibid, p.226
[64] Trevor, Hugh. (Undated) *Japan's Post-War Protestant Churches*, p.14. Unpublished – kept by OMF Japan
[65] Fujiwara, Atsuyoshi. (2012) *Theology of Culture in a Japanese Context*, p.235. Oregon: Pickwick Publications
[66] Ibid, p.236
[67] Parker, Calvin. F. (1998) Christ in a Kimono, p.136. USA: Morris Publishing
[68] Trevor, Hugh. (Undated) *Japan's Post-War Protestant Churches*, p.16. Unpublished – kept by OMF Japan
[69] Ibid, p.16
[70] Lee, Samuel C. (2011) *Understanding Japan: Through the eyes of Christian faith. Fourth Edition*, p.23. Amsterdam: Foundation University Press
[71] Fujiwara, Atsuyoshi. (2012) *Theology of Culture in a Japanese Context*, p.276. Oregon: Pickwick Publications
[72] Trevor, Hugh. (Undated) *Japan's Post-War Protestant Churches*, p.16-17. Unpublished – kept by OMF Japan
[73] Ibid, p.17
[74] Ibid, p.19 20
[75] Ibid, p.22
[76] Ibid, p.26-28
[77] Mehn, John Wm. (2017) *Multiplying Churches in Japanese Soil*, p. xvii. Pasadena: William Carey Library
[78] Endo, Shusaku. (Translated by William Johnston) (1969) *Silence*, p.205. USA: Picador Modern Classics (2016)
[79] Mehn, John Wm. (2017) *Multiplying Churches in Japanese Soil*, p.49. Pasadena: William Carey Library
[80] Joshua Project. (2019) 'Unreached Listings: 100 Largest Unreached Peoples'. Frontier Ventures. Accessed on 1st April 2019 at:
https://joshuaproject.net/unreached/1?limit=100&s=Population&o=asc
[81] Mehn, John Wm. (2017) *Multiplying Churches in Japanese Soil*, p. xv-xvi. Pasadena: William Carey Library
[82] Lee, Samuel C. (2011) *Understanding Japan: Through the eyes of Christian faith. Fourth Edition*, p.90. Amsterdam: Foundation University Press
[83] Mehn, John Wm. (2017) *Multiplying Churches in Japanese Soil*, p.7. Pasadena: William Carey Library

[84] Lewis, David. C. (1993) *The Unseen Face of Japan*, p.294. UK: Monarch
[85] Ibid, p.271
[86] Ibid, p.279
[87] Ibid, p.291
[88] Mehn, John Wm. (2017) *Multiplying Churches in Japanese Soil*, p.28. Pasadena: William Carey Library
[89] Ibid, p.32
[90] Lee, Samuel C. (2011) *Understanding Japan: Through the eyes of Christian faith. Fourth Edition*, p.145. Amsterdam: Foundation University Press
[91] Lewis, David. C. (1993) *The Unseen Face of Japan*, p.287-290. UK: Monarch
[92] Mehn, John Wm. (2017) *Multiplying Churches in Japanese Soil*, p.17. Pasadena: William Carey Library
[93] Lewis, David. C. (1993) *The Unseen Face of Japan*, p.276-277. UK: Monarch
[94] Gosden, Eric. (1982). *The Other Ninety-Nine*, p.44-45. London: Marshalls Paperbacks & The Japan Evangelistic Band
[95] Ibid, p.42
[96] Lee, Samuel C. (2011) *Understanding Japan: Through the eyes of Christian faith. Fourth Edition*, p.92. Amsterdam: Foundation University Press
[97] Mehn, John Wm. (2017) *Multiplying Churches in Japanese Soil*, p. xviii. Pasadena: William Carey Library
[98] Ferreira in Endo, Shusaku. (Translated by William Johnston) (1969) *Silence*, p.198. USA: Picador Modern Classics (2016)

Glossary

Attrition

Attrition means wearing down and missionary attrition has been defined "in its broadest sense as departure from service...regardless of cause. However, our prime concerns...speak to the causes of premature or painful departure."[1]

Buddhism/Buddhist

Japanese Buddhism emphasises freedom from pain and rewards for good deeds.[2] It includes Zen Buddhist values such as obligation, sacrifice, and perseverance.[3] It is also influenced by Confucianism[4] and embraces ancestor worship.[5]

Burnout

O'Donnell defined burnout as "the incapacitating result of emotional distress and behavioural dysfunction due to chronic, unresolved stress."[6] Similarly, Dodds described burnout as "resulting from prolonged and total depletion of a person's resources...The person has been 'used up'."[7]

Confucianism

Confucianism promotes a harmonious, ritualistic, and hierarchical society[8] expressed through practices like filial piety, status-related forms of address, and bowing.[9] De Mente described this as showing and preserving harmony in the social order and the cosmos.[10] This leads to conformity, group consciousness[11], and social harmony (*wa*).

Debriefing

"Debriefing is telling our story, complete with experiences and feelings, from our point of view. It is a verbal processing of past events...an opportunity to share in depth recent experiences with someone who is willing to listen and care, without judgement or criticism."[12] Debriefing is an optional, relatively brief exercise done for the benefit of the individual, rather than their organisation. In contrast, counselling seeks to alleviate long-term issues and is usually conducted over a longer period than debriefing.

Enculturation

Enculturation means learning the culture of a group, through education, observation and involvement.

High-retaining agency

High-retaining mission agencies are those with a good record in keeping or retaining missionaries in their service. This terminology is used in ReMAP II (see entry below).[13]

Home assignment/home leave/furlough

Home assignment, home leave, and furlough all refer to periods when missionaries return to their home or sending countries to speak about their work, raise financial support, and inspire others in the global missionary task. Home assignments vary greatly in length (typically 1–12 months) and occur every 1–4 years, depending on the missionary, their agency, and their family situation.

Japan Church Planting Institute (JCPI; http://jcpi.net/)

The Japan Church Planting Institute (JCPI) (often referred to as simply the Church Planting Institute or CPI) began in 1994 as a ministry of the Japan Evangelical Missionary Association (JEMA). JCPI is a cooperative effort by missions, missionaries, and Japanese leaders and workers to see indigenous, gospel-driven, church planting movements fostered in Japan.

Japan Evangelical Missionary Association (JEMA; http://www.jema.org)

The Japan Evangelical Missionary Association (JEMA) is an association of individuals and mission agencies in Japan that is seeking to help network and equip its members to make disciples for Christ. JEMA's ministries currently consist of member care, women in ministry, and prayer. JEMA also produces a quarterly magazine written by and for members called *Japan Harvest*.

Long-term service

Long-term service is difficult to define. For early missionary pioneers, long term meant for life. More recently, long term often means more than three or four years. ReMAP II found that in the years 2001–2002, the average length of missionary service in high-retaining mission agencies was 15.5 years and 7.9 years in low-retaining mission agencies.[14] However, considering that missionaries have to learn the Japanese language and culture, which are known for being challenging, and gain competency in ministry, I believe a minimum of 10 years of missionary service is appropriate in the Japanese context (for as long as God calls).

Low-retaining agency

Low-retaining (mission) agencies are those with a poor record in keeping or retaining missionaries in their service. This terminology is used in ReMAP II (see entry below).[15]

Meiji Constitution

The Meiji Constitution (1889 to 1947) developed out of the Meiji Restoration (1868), as Japanese leaders wanted to show Japan as a capable, modern nation, deserving the respect of Western nations, while maintaining its own power.[16]

Meiji Restoration

The Meiji Restoration was a political revolution in 1868, which brought about industrialisation, modernisation, Westernisation, and increased nationalism in Japan. It brought the Tokugawa Shogunate to an end and returned the country to direct imperial rule under Emperor Meiji.[17][18]

Member care

Member care is described by O'Donnell as "the ongoing investment of resources by…agencies, churches, and other mission organizations for the nurture and development of…personnel. It focuses on everyone in missions…over the course of the missionary life cycle."[19] The Global Member Care Network adds "Member Care is doing whatever it takes…to insure that our workers feel cared for and supported…that they have the resources…to work effectively, and to care…for themselves and their family."[20]

Ministry mismatch

I define this as a sense of not fitting or suiting the ministry or role in which a missionary is placed, as manifested by internal feelings of discomfort or the external reality of an inability to fulfil the role.

QDA Miner (Lite)

QDA Miner is computer-assisted qualitative analysis software and is available in paid or free versions (QDA Miner Lite). I used this software to analyse the vast quantity of textual information gained from my interviews, by using the coding functions and producing graphs to illustrate my findings. Website: https://provalisresearch.com/products/qualitative-data-analysis-software/freeware/

ReMAP (I)

The Reducing Missionary Attrition Project (ReMAP) (1995) surveyed 455 mission agencies representing 23,000 missionaries.[21] ReMAP's results were published in the book *Too Valuable to Lose: Exploring the Causes and Cures of Missionary Attrition*.[22]

ReMAP II

ReMAP II (Retaining Missionaries: Agency Practices) (2002) collected data from 22 countries and 600 agencies representing nearly 40,000 missionaries.[23] ReMAP II's results were published in the book *Worth Keeping: Global Perspectives on Best Practice in Missionary Retention*.[24]

Resilience

O'Donnell described resilience as "a person's ability to cope with challenges and difficulties…to resolve and maintain a new balance when the old one is challenged or destroyed."[25] Blanchetière noted that resilience involves learning from tough situations.[26] Carr described resilience as "having strength to fulfil the call God has given…even when it will be painful and difficult…staying fixed on a higher purpose."[27] I define resilience as a process of positive change in and through adversity, relying on God's power at work within the individual, in order to fulfil God's calling.[28]

Retention

The World Evangelical Alliance defined retention as "the ability of an agency to keep its people."[29] Van Meter commented, "Retention is more than the opposite of attrition. Retention takes into consideration who…people are…how long they have been with the agency, at what point…a person leaves, and the reasons for…leaving."[30]

Shinto/Shintoism

Shintoism is animistic, with no explicit moral code or concept of sin.[31] Worshippers seek blessing and protection from many gods[32] and revere nature, but without the concept of a Creator.

Spiritual warfare

"Put on the full armour of God, so that you can take your stand against the devil's schemes. For our struggle is not against flesh and blood, but against the rulers, against the authorities, against the powers of this dark world and against the spiritual forces of evil in the heavenly realms." (Ephesians 6:11–12; NIV) "Spiritual warfare is the leveraging of everything that God promises against everything that opposes God's purposes."[33] Mehn has discussed spiritual resistance in Japan, saying "the main hindrance…in Japan is not just conceptual, cultural, or practical but ultimately spiritual."[34]

Stress

O'Donnell described stress as "the response of the entire person spiritually, emotionally, physically, socially to internal and external demands."[35] However, Backus' perspective is helpful as he says, "Stress is not something that happens to us…stress is the way we respond to what happens…What we tell ourselves about the event is what makes an event stressful."[36]

Survey Monkey

Survey Monkey is a survey design and distribution application that has both free and paid versions. I used the paid version to design, distribute, analyse, and present my survey data. Website: https://www.surveymonkey.com/

Syncretism/syncretistic

Syncretism means combining different religious beliefs and practices. It has been said that in Japan, Shinto is the tree roots, the heart of the Japanese; Confucianism is the trunk and branches, the politics, morality and education; and Buddhism is the flowering of religious feelings.[37] This highly syncretistic worldview pervades Japanese thought and action.

Taoism/Taoist

Tao means "way", signifying a doctrine and code of behaviour. In Japanese, this word is *dō*, found in words like *sadō* (tea ceremony), *shodō* (calligraphy), and *bushidō* (the way of the warrior).[38] Taoism combines sacred forces with rituals.[39] To communicate with the sacred, one simply follows rituals like those of the tea ceremony, for example.[40]

Taylor, William D. (2002) 'Revisiting a Provocative Theme: The Attrition of Longer-Term Missionaries', *Missiology* 30 Issue 1, p.67. Accessed on 13th June 2018 at: http://journals.sagepub.com/doi/pdf/10.1177/009182960203000105

Ayabe, Henry. (1992) *Step Inside*, p.122. Tokyo: Japan Evangelical Missionary Association

De Mente, Boyé Lafayette. (2004) *The Japanese Samurai Code*, p.9. USA and Japan: Tuttle Publishing

Cortazzi, Hugh. (1994) *Modern Japan: A Concise Survey*, p.8. Japan: The Japan Times

Davies, Roger J. (2016) *Japanese Culture: The Religious and Philosophical Foundations*, p.36. USA, Singapore & Japan: Tuttle Publishing

[6] O'Donnell, Kelly. (2011) *Global Member Care: The Pearls and Perils of Good Practice*, p.27. Pasadena, CA, USA: William Carey Library

[7] Dodds, L&L quoted by Bosch, Brenda. (2014) *Thriving in Difficult Places: Member Care for Yourself and Others – Volume 1*, p.59. Self-Published by the author. www.thrivingmember.com

[8] Cortazzi, Hugh. (1994) *Modern Japan: A Concise Survey*, p.7. Japan: The Japan Times

[9] Benedict, Ruth. (1946) *The Chrysanthemum and the Sword*, p.47-51. USA & Japan: Tuttle Publishing (2000)

[10] De Mente, Boyé Lafayette. (2003) *Kata: The Key to Understanding & Dealing with the Japanese*, p.1. USA and Japan: Tuttle Publishing

[11] De Mente, Boyé Lafayette. (2008) *Etiquette Guide to Japan*, p.16. USA and Japan: Tuttle Publishing

[12] Williams, K quoted by Bosch, Brenda. (2014) *Thriving in Difficult Places: Member Care for Yourself and Others – Volume 1*, p.153. Self-Published by the author. www.thrivingmember.com

[13] Bloecher, Detlef. (2004) 'Good Agency Practices: Lessons from ReMAP II'. *Connections: The Journal of the WEA Missions Commission*, 3 (2), p.12-25. Accessed on 13th June 2018 at: http://worldevangelicals.org/resources/rfiles/res3_124_link_1292364866.pdf

[14] ReMAP II – Retaining Missionaries – Agency Practices (Older Sending Countries) (PowerPoint), Slide #31

[15] Bloecher, Detlef. (2004) 'Good Agency Practices: Lessons from ReMAP II'. *Connections: The Journal of the WEA Missions Commission*, 3 (2), p.12-25. Accessed on 13th June 2018 at: http://worldevangelicals.org/resources/rfiles/res3_124_link_1292364866.pdf

[16] Encyclopaedia Britannica. Accessed on 27th May 2020 at: https://www.britannica.com/topic/Meiji-Constitution

[17] Fujiwara, Atsuyoshi. (2012) *Theology of Culture in a Japanese Context*, p.211. Oregon: Pickwick Publications)

[18] Encyclopaedia Britannica. Accessed on 27th May 2020 at: https://www.britannica.com/event/Meiji-Restoration

[19] O'Donnell, Kelly. (ed.) (2002) *Doing Member Care Well*, p.4. California: William Carey Library

[20] Quoted by Gardner, Laura Mae. (2015) *Healthy Resilient, and Effective in Cross-Cultural Ministry – A Comprehensive Member Care Plan*, p.15. Indonesia: Katalis gloria

[21] Thompson, Craig. (2017) *Is Conflict with Teammates Really the Top Reason for Missionaries Leaving the Field?* Accessed on 12th June 2018 at: http://www.alifeoverseas.com/is-conflict-with-teammates-really-the-top-reason-for-missionaries-leaving-the-field/ and Bloecher, Detlef. (2005) 'Reducing Missionary Attrition (ReMAP) - what it said and what it did', p.1-2. Accessed on 26th May 2021 at: Microsoft Word - ReMAPI summary.doc (dmgint.de)

[22] Taylor, William D. (1997) *Too Valuable to Lose*, p. xv. Pasadena: William Carey Library.

[23] Hay, R. et al. (2007) *Worth Keeping: Global Perspectives on Best Practices in Missionary Retention*, p.23, 30. Pasadena, Calif.: William Carey Library

[24] Ibid.

[25] O'Donnell, Kelly. (2013) *Global Member Care: Crossing Sectors for Serving Humanity*, p.337. Pasadena, CA, USA: William Carey Library

[26] Blanchetière, Pascale. (2006) 'Resilience of Humanitarian Workers', p.3. Accessed on 8th April 2021 at: https://www.alnap.org/system/files/content/resource/files/main/resilience-of-aid-workers-article.pdf

[27] Carr, Karen F. in Schaefer, Frauke C & Schaefer, Charles A. (2012) *Trauma & Resilience: A Handbook*, p.93. Self-published by the authors.

[28] Dallman, J. (2018). 'Analyse the concept of resilience and its significance within a declared cultural context. Assess the ways of handling it suggested in the course and/or covered in the recommended literature. Conclude with reasoned and innovative applications for an integrated approach to your practice of Member Care.'p.3. Unpublished.

[29] World Evangelical Alliance (Missions Commission). (2010) *ReMAP II: Worldwide Missionary Retention Study & Best Practices*, p.38. Accessed on: 2nd August 2018 at: http://www.worldevangelicals.org/resources/rfiles/res3_96_link_1292358945.pdf

[30] Van Meter, Jim. (2003) *US Report of Findings on Missionary Retention*, p.2. Accessed on 14th June 2018 at: http://www.worldevangelicals.org/resources/rfiles/res3_95_link_1292358708.pdf

[31] Lee, Samuel C. (2011) *Understanding Japan: Through the eyes of Christian faith*. Fourth Edition, p.92. Amsterdam: Foundation University Press

[32] Gosden, Eric. (1982). *The Other Ninety-Nine*, p.41. London: Marshalls Paperbacks & The Japan Evangelistic Band

[33] Intervarsity. 'What Spiritual Warfare Is (and What It Definitely Isn't)', no page. Accessed on 27th May 2020 at: https://intervarsity.org/blog/what-spiritual-warfare-and-what-it-definitely-isn't

[34] Mehn, John Wm. (2017) *Multiplying Churches in Japanese Soil*, p.17. Pasadena: William Carey Library

[35] O'Donnell, Kelly. (2011) *Global Member Care: The Pearls and Perils of Good Practice*, p.27. Pasadena, CA, USA: William Carey Library

[36] Backus (1996) quoted by Bosch, Brenda. (2014) *Thriving in Difficult Places: Member Care for Yourself and Others – Volume 1*, p.7. Self-Published by the author. www.thrivingmember.com

[37] Davies, Roger J. (2016) *Japanese Culture: The Religious and Philosophical Foundations*, p.39. USA, Singapore & Japan: Tuttle Publishing

[38] Ibid, p.80.

[39] Ibid, p.80.

[40] Ibid, p.81.

Bibliography

Adiwardana, M.N. (2006) 'Training Missionaries to Persevere in Situations of Adversity', *Mission Round Table: The Occasional Bulletin of OMF Mission Research 2(2),* pp.11-15 Accessed on 13th June 2018 at:
https://www.groupconnection.net/irj/go/km/docs/room_extensions/cm_stores/documents/workspaces/e0e88eda-77a6-3110-d7bf-ba64a07de65d/Mission%20Round%20Table/MRT%20-%20PDFs%20of%20individual%20articles/MRT%2002.2%20Training%20to%20persevere%20in%20adversity%20-%20Margaretha%20Adiwardana.pdf

Allen, Frank. (1986) 'Why Do They Leave? Reflections on Attrition', *Evangelical Missions Quarterly,* 22 no. 2 Apr 1986, p 118-129. Accessed on 7th May 2018 at: https://missionexus.org/why-do-they-leave-reflections-on-attrition/

Ash, Christopher. (2016) *Zeal without Burnout.* UK & USA: The Good Book Company

Ayabe, Henry. (1992) *Step Inside.* Tokyo: Japan Evangelical Missionary Association

Barclay, John S. (2010) *Families in Cross-Cultural Ministry: a comprehensive guide and manual for families, administrators and supporters.* Unpublished Doctor of Ministry thesis: Australian College of Theology

BBC News. (2018) *Aum Shinrikyo: Images from the 1995 Tokyo Sarin attack.* Accessed on 2nd July 2019 at: https://www.bbc.com/news/in-pictures-43629706

Benedict, Ruth. (1946) *The Chrysanthemum and the Sword.* USA & Japan: Tuttle Publishing (2000)

Bergman, Jesse. (2014) *Calculate Mean Median and Mode for Grouped Data.* Accessed on 27th June 2019 at: https://www.youtube.com/watch?v=lXPvC8D_ptE

Blanchetière, Pascale. (2006) 'Resilience of Humanitarian Workers', p.3. Accessed on 8th April 2021 at:
https://www.alnap.org/system/files/content/resource/files/main/resilience-of-aid-workers-article.pdf

Bloecher, Detlef. (2005) 'ReMAP II – Retaining Missionaries – Agency Practices: Newer sending countries from Africa, Asia and Latin America'. Accessed on 26th May 2021 at: 1 ReMAP II – Retaining Missionaries – Agency Practices Newer sending countries from Africa, Asia and Latin America. - ppt download (slideplayer.com)

Bloecher, Detlef. (2005) 'ReMAP II – Retaining Missionaries – Agency Practices: Older sending countries in Europe and North America'. Accessed on 26th May 2021 at: 1 ReMAP II – Retaining Missionaries – Agency Practices Older sending countries in Europe and North America. - ppt download (slideplayer.com)

Bloecher, Detlef. (2005) 'Reducing Missionary Attrition (ReMAP) - what it said and what it did'. Accessed on 26th May 2021 at: Microsoft Word - ReMAPI summary.doc (dmgint.de)

Bloecher, Detlef. (2004) 'Good Agency Practices: Lessons from ReMAP II'. *Connections: The Journal of the WEA Missions Commission, 3 (2)*, p.12-25. Accessed on 13th June 2018 at: http://worldevangelicals.org/resources/rfiles/res3_124_link_1292364866.pdf

Bloecher, Detlef. (No date) 'Good agency practices – lessons from ReMAP II'. Accessed on 26th May 2021 at: Good Agency Practices: Lessons from ReMAP II - Missio Nexus

Bosch, Brenda. (2014) *Thriving in Difficult Places: Member Care for Yourself and Others – Volume 1*. Self-Published by the author. www.thrivingmember.com

Bosch, Brenda. (2014) *Thriving in Difficult Places: Member Care for Yourself and Others – Volume 2*. Self-Published by the author. www.thrivingmember.com

Bosch, Brenda. (2014) *Thriving in Difficult Places: Member Care for Yourself and Others – Volume 3*. Self-Published by the author. www.thrivingmember.com

Brierley, Peter. (1996) *Mission Attrition: Why Missionaries Return Home*. London: Christian Research

Brierley, Peter. (1996) *Mission Attrition: Why Missionaries Return Home – Appendix Tables*. London: Christian Research

Brown, Ronald. (2006) 'Preparing for the Realities of Missions in a Changing World', *Evangelical Missions Quarterly* October- December 2006, Volume 42, Issue 4. Accessed on 9th April 2021 at: Preparing for the Realities of Missions in a Changing World - Missio Nexus

Brown, Ronald. (2005) 'Resilience in Ministry despite Trauma'. Mobile Member Care Team. Accessed on 13th November 2017 at: http://storage.cloversites.com/mmctmobilemembercareteam/documents/Resilience%20i n%20Ministry%20Despite%20Trauma.pdf

Bylund, Emanuel, Abrahamsson, Niclas & Hyltenstam, Kenneth. (2010) 'The Role of Language Aptitude in First Language Attrition: The Case of Pre-pubescent Attriters', *Applied Linguistics 31:3*, UK: Oxford University Press

Carmichael, Amy. (1987) *Fragments that remain*. The Dohnavur Fellowship. CLC Publications, e-book 2013.

Carr, Karen F. & Schaefer, Frauke C. (2010) 'Trauma and Traumatic Stress in Cross-cultural Missions: How to Promote Resilience', *Evangelical Missions Quarterly* Vol. 46, No.3, pp.278-285 Accessed on 26th May 2021 at: Trauma and Traumatic Stress in Cross-cultural Missions: How to Promote Resilience - Missio Nexus

Center for the Study of Global Christianity. (2019) 'Status of Global Christianity, 2019, in the Context of 1900-2050'. Accessed on 23rd July 2019 at: https://gordonconwell.edu/wp-content/uploads/sites/13/2019/04/StatusofGlobalChristianity20191.pdf

Charmaz, Kathy. (2004) 'Grounded Theory', *The SAGE Encyclopedia of Social Science Research Methods*, Sage Research Methods, Sage Publications Inc.

Christian Shinbun (クリスチャン新聞), *Christian Data Book 2018* (クリスチャン情報ブック 2018)　Inochi no Kotoba (いのちのことば社), Japan.

Clements, Jonathan. (2017) *A Brief History of Japan: Samurai, Shogun and Zen: The Extraordinary Story of the Land of the Rising Sun*. USA, Singapore & Japan: Tuttle Publishing

Cortazzi, Hugh. (1994) *Modern Japan: A Concise Survey*. Japan: The Japan Times

Cottrell, Stella. (2014) *Dissertations and Project Reports: A step by step guide*. UK/USA: Palgrave Macmillan

Creswell John W. (2013) *Qualitative Inquiry & Research Design: Choosing Among Five Approaches*. 3rd revised edition. Los Angeles/London/New Delhi/Singapore/Washington DC: SAGE Publications, Inc.

Creswell, John W. (2014) *Research design: qualitative, quantitative, and mixed methods approaches*. 4th edition. Los Angeles/London/New Delhi/Singapore/Washington DC: SAGE Publications, Inc.

Crossley-Baxter, Lily. (2018) 'Japan's unusual way to view the world.' Accessed on 30th October 2018 at: http://www.bbc.com/travel/story/20181021-japans-unusual-way-to-view-the-world

Crotty Michael. (2015) *Foundations of Social Research*. Los Angeles/London/New Delhi/Singapore/Washington DC: Sage Publications Ltd

Dallman, Janet. (2019) *Factors affecting missionary attrition and retention in Japan*. MA in Member Care for Redcliffe College, UK. Unpublished.

Dallman, Janet. (2016) *Out on a Limb*, USA, Xulon Publishing.

David, R. (2019) 'Editorial: Elder Member Care', Global Member Care Network (GMCN) March 2019. Accessed on 7th May 2020 at https://www.facebook.com/groups/globalmembercare/

Davies, Roger J. (2016) *Japanese Culture: The Religious and Philosophical Foundations*. USA, Singapore & Japan: Tuttle Publishing.

Davies, Roger J. & Ikeno, Osamu. (2002) *The Japanese Mind: Understanding Contemporary Japanese Culture*. USA, Singapore & Japan: Tuttle Publishing.

De Mente, Boyé Lafayette. (2008) *Etiquette Guide to Japan*. USA and Japan: Tuttle Publishing

De Mente, Boyé Lafayette. (2004) *The Japanese Samurai Code*. USA and Japan: Tuttle Publishing

De Mente, Boyé Lafayette. (2003) *Kata: The Key to Understanding & Dealing with the Japanese*. USA and Japan: Tuttle Publishing

Dodds, Lois. A. & Dodds, Lawrence. E. (1999) *Love and Survival: In Life, In Missions*. (Part of Collected Papers on the Care of Missionaries 2000) Pennsylvania: Heartstream Resources

Doi, Takeo. (1973) *The Anatomy of Dependence*. USA: Kodansha America

Doughill, John. (2016) *In Search of Japan's Hidden Christians*. UK: SPCK

Edwards, Colin. (Unknown) 'Grounded Theory and Coding.' Webinar, Redcliffe College. Accessed on 24th April 2018. No longer available.

Eenigenburg, Sue & Bliss, Robynn. (2010) *Expectations and Burnout: Women Surviving the Great Commission*. California: William Carey Library

Effective Language Learning. (2017) Accessed on: 26th December 2017 at: http://www.effectivelanguagelearning.com/language-guide/language-difficulty

Endo, Shusaku. (Translated by William Johnston) (1969) *Silence*. USA: Picador Modern Classics (2016).

Evans, Richard & Louisa. (2016) 'Building Resilience in Mission.' Accessed on 19th December 2017 at: http://www.globalconnections.org.uk/sites/newgc.localhost/files/papers/ihr_forum_event_may_2016_-_building_resilience_in_mission_ppt_-_richard_and_louisa_evans.pdf

Fawcett, Graham. (1999) *Ad-mission: The Briefing and Debriefing of Team of Missionaries and Aid Workers*. Great Britain: Youth With A Mission

Fawcett, John. (ed.) (2003) *Stress and Trauma Handbook: Strategies for Flourishing in Demanding Environments*. California: World Vision International

Fluid Surveys University. (2014) 'Presenting Your Rating Scales -Numbered versus Worded Lists', Accessed on 10th September 2018 at: http://fluidsurveys.com/university/number-versus-word-rating-scales/

Fluid Surveys University. (2014) 'Odd or Even? –The Ongoing Debate of Neutral Rating Scales', Accessed on 10th September 2018 at: http://fluidsurveys.com/university/odds-evens-ongoing-debate-rating-scale/

Foyle, Marjory. (2001) *Honourably Wounded: Stress among Christian Workers*. Rev. ed. London: Monarch Books.

Fujimura, Makoto. (2016) *Silence and Beauty: Hidden Faith Born of Suffering*. Illinois: IVP

Fujiwara, Atsuyoshi. (2012) *Theology of Culture in a Japanese Context*. Oregon: Pickwick Publications

Fullerton, Mark A. (2010) *A Missional Reading of the Psalms of Lament: Exploring the Implications of the Lamenting Psalms as Preventative Measure for Western Missionary Attrition in the 21st Century*. Unpublished thesis: Redcliffe College

Gallup Inc. (2018) 'Live Your Best Life Using CliftonStrengths'. Accessed on 21st May 2019 at: https://www.gallupstrengthscenter.com/?gclid=EAIaIQobChMIlryn3O-P4gIVmwQqCh3ECACfEAAYASAAEgLY9vD_BwE

Gardner, Larrie and Lindquist, Brent. (2012) *Setting the Stage: A Global Member Care Conversation*. Condeo Press

Gardner, Laura Mae. (2015) *Healthy Resilient, and Effective in Cross-Cultural Ministry – A Comprehensive Member Care Plan*. Indonesia: Katalis gloria

Gardener, Laura Mae. (1987) 'Proactive Care of Missionary Personnel', *Journal of Psychology & Theology* Volume 15:4. Accessed on 14th June 2018 at: http://web.b.ebscohost.com/ehost/pdfviewer/pdfviewer?vid=3&sid=f75ea4c3-f71a-464d-892c-e5a0374d5c3d%40pdc-v-sessmgr01

Gibbs, Graham. R. (2010) 'Coding Part 1: Alan Bryman's four stages of qualitative analysis'. University of Huddersfield. Accessed on 24th April 2018 at: https://www.youtube.com/watch?v=7X7VuQxPfpk

Gibbs, Graham. R. (2010) 'Coding Part 2: Thematic Coding'. University of Huddersfield. Accessed on 24th April 2018 at: https://www.youtube.com/watch?v=B_YXR9kp1_o

Gibbs, Graham. R. (2010) 'Coding Part 3: What can codes be about?' University of Huddersfield. Accessed on 24th April 2018 at: https://www.youtube.com/watch?v=3oo8ZcBJIEY

Gibbs, Graham. R. (2010) 'Coding Part 4: What is coding for?' University of Huddersfield. Accessed on 24th April 2018 at: https://www.youtube.com/watch?v=5xM-9yuBhMc

Gibbs, Graham. R. (2010) 'Coding Part 5: The code list or code hierarchy'. University of Huddersfield. Accessed on 24th April 2018 at: https://www.youtube.com/watch?v=DVpkuTdkZvA

Gordon, Andrew. (2014) *A Modern History of Japan*. Third Edition. New York & Oxford: Oxford University Press

Gosden, Eric. (1982). *The Other Ninety-Nine*. London: Marshalls Paperbacks & The Japan Evangelistic Band

Grand Canyon University. (No date). 'Phenomenology Research Overview'. Accessed on 7th June 2019 at: https://cirt.gcu.edu/research/developmentresources/research_ready/phenomenology/phen_overview

Guthrie, Stan. (2000) *Missions in the Third Millennium: 21 Key Trends for the 21st Century*. UK & USA: Paternoster Press

Hale, Thomas & Daniels, Gene. (2012) *On Being a Missionary (Revised Edition)*. California: William Carey Library

Hay, Rob, Valerie Lim, Detlef Blöcher, Jaap Ketelaar, and Sarah Hay. (2007) *Worth Keeping: Global Perspectives on Best Practices in Missionary Retention*. Pasadena, Calif.: William Carey Library

Hendry, Joy. (2013) *Understanding Japanese Society*. (Fourth Edition). London and New York: Routledge

Hibbert, Richard & Evelyn. (2013) 'Is It Time? How to Know When It's Time to Leave the Field'. *Evangelical Missions Quarterly 49:2* Accessed on 26th May 2021 at: Is It Time? How to Know When It's Time to Leave the Field - Missio Nexus

Hoke, Steve & Taylor, Bill. (2009) *Global Mission Handbook: A Guide for Crosscultural Service*. Illinois: IVP

Horsfall, Tony. (2017) 'Resilience in life and ministry' (Power Point) Accessed on 13th November 2017 at: https://graceworks.com.sg/wp-content/uploads/Resilience-in-Life-and-Ministry.pdf

Ingleby, Sue. (2017) 'Stress and Burnout among Mission Workers' (extract), Redcliffe College, UK.

Intervarsity. 'What Spiritual Warfare Is (and What It Definitely Isn't)'. Accessed on 27th May 2020 at: https://intervarsity.org/blog/what-spiritual-warfare-and-what-it-definitely-isn't

Japan Evangelical Missionary Association. (2018) *JEMA Directory 2018*. Japan

Jones, Michael & Elizabeth (ed.). (1996) *Caring for the Missionary into the 21st Century II: Papers from the 1996 Conference*, UK: Care for Mission

Jones, Michael (ed.). (1993) *Caring for the Missionary into the 21st Century: Papers presented at a 1993 seminar*. UK: Care for Mission

Jordan, Peter. (1992) *Re-Entry*. USA: Youth With A Mission Publishing

Joshua Project. (2019) 'Unreached Listings: 100 Largest Unreached Peoples'. Frontier Ventures. Accessed on 1st April 2019 at:
https://joshuaproject.net/unreached/1?limit=100&a=Population&co=asc

Joshua Project. (2019) 'Global Mission Trends'. Accessed on 23rd July 2019 at: https://joshuaproject.net/assets/media/handouts/global-mission-trends.pdf

Kent, Martha, Davis, Mary. C, Reich, John. W. (ed.) (2014) *The Resilience Handbook: Approaches to Stress and Trauma*. New York & London: Routledge

Kingston, Jeff. (2013) *Contemporary Japan: History, Politics & Social Change Since the 1980s*. UK: John Wiley & Sons Ltd

Knell, Marion. (2007) *Burn-up or Splash Down*. USA: Authentic Publishing

Koteskey, Ron. (2011) 'What Missionaries Ought to Know about Premature Departure from the Field'. Wilmore, Ken.: New Hope International Ministries. Accessed on 9th April 2018 at: http://www.missionarycare.com/attrition.html

Kvale, Steinar and Brinkmann Svend. (2009) *InterViews: Learning the Craft of Qualitative Research Interviewing*. 2nd edition. Los Angeles/London/New Delhi/Singapore/Washington DC: Sage Publications Inc.

Lane, Edwin. (2017) 'The young Japanese working themselves to death'. Accessed on 1st January 2018 at: http://www.bbc.com/news/business-39981997

Lanier, Miriam L. (2018) *Member care for workers in Lebanon: Toward understanding their unique needs and assessing the provision of member care*. MA in Member Care thesis: Redcliffe College. Accessed on 29th October 2018 at: https://online.redcliffe.ac.uk/pluginfile.php/16982/mod_page/content/71/Lanier%2C%20Miriam%20dissertation%202018%20MAMC.pdf

Lee, Samuel C. (2014) *The Japanese and Christianity: Why Is Christianity Not Widely Believed in Japan?* Amsterdam: Foundation University Press.

Lee, Samuel C. (2011) *Understanding Japan: Through the eyes of Christian faith*. Fourth Edition. Amsterdam: Foundation University Press.

Lee, Samuel C. (2010) *Rediscovering Japan: Reintroducing Christendom*. Maryland: Hamilton Books

Lewis, David. C. (1993) *The Unseen Face of Japan*. UK: Monarch.

Littler, Julian. (2019). 'The Art of Perseverance: How gaman defined Japan.' Accessed on 27th March 2019 at: http://www.bbc.com/capital/story/20190319-the-art-of-perseverance-how-gaman-defined-japan?ocid=ww.social.link.facebook&fbclid=IwAR2fEZAzc71AxgQ-Wc8RwO-IQ7a-wdeg7MGCGF6H4pRQ38hvZnZ3CB-bIeI

Mason, R.H.P. & Caiger, J.G. (1997) *A History of Japan*. Revised Edition. Japan, USA & Singapore: Tuttle Publishing

McMillan, Kathleen and Weyers, Jonathan. (2008) *How to Write Dissertations & Project Reports*. England: Pearson Education Limited

Mehn, John Wm. (2017) *Multiplying Churches in Japanese Soil*. Pasadena: William Carey Library.

Merriam-Webster Incorporated. (1997) *Merriam-Webster's Collegiate Dictionary*. Tenth Edition. USA: Merriam-Webster Incorporated.

Missiographics. 'Going the Distance: Missionary Retention'. (No date) Accessed on 9th April 2018 at: https://visual.ly/community/infographic/lifestyle/missionary-retention

Myers & Briggs Foundation (The). (2019) 'MBTI Basics' Florida, USA. Accessed on 21st May 2019 at: https://www.myersbriggs.org/my-mbti-personality-type/mbti-basics/home.htm?bhcp=1

Nakane, Chie. (1970) *Japanese Society*. California: University of California.

Nelson, James. (2015) 'Excellence in Missions: Four Ways to Improve Field Staff Retention', *Evangelical Missions Quarterly*, Vol. 51, No. 4 pp.440-445 Accessed on 8th June 2021 at: EMQ_Volume_51_Issue_4.pdf

Nelson, James. (2010) 'The Engage! Study Executive Summary', *Evangelical Missions Quarterly* Volume 46:3, Accessed on 8th June 2021 at: The Engage! Study Executive Summary - Missio Nexus

O'Donnell, Kelly. (2013) *Global Member Care: Crossing Sectors for Serving Humanity*. Pasadena, CA, USA: William Carey Library

O'Donnell, Kelly. (2011) *Global Member Care: The Pearls and Perils of Good Practice*. Pasadena, CA, USA: William Carey Library

O'Donnell, Kelly. (ed.) (2002) *Doing Member Care Well*. California: William Carey Library

O'Donnell, Kelly. (ed.) (1992) *Missionary Care: counting the cost for world evangelization*. California: William Carey Library

O'Donnell, Kelly S. and Michele Lewis. (ed.) (1998) *Helping Missionaries Grow*. California: William Carey Library

No author named except 'Dave'. (2015) *The sad facts about missionary attrition*. Accessed on 14th June 2018 at: https://paracletos.org/the-sad-facts-about-missionary-attrition/

Parker, Calvin. F. (1998) *Christ in a Kimono*. USA: Morris Publishing

Parkhill, Beverlea. (2018) *Self-Care for Single Mission Workers within OMF International (UK): The Challenges and Opportunities*. MA in Member Care thesis: Redcliffe College. Accessed on 29th October 2018 at: https://online.redcliffe.ac.uk/pluginfile.php/16982/mod_page/content/71/Parkhill%2C%20Beverlea%20dissertation%202018%20MAMC.pdf

Pirolo, Neal. (2000) *The Reentry Team*. USA: Emmaus Road International

Powell, John. R. & Bowers, Joyce. M. (2002) *Enhancing Missionary Vitality*. Colorado: Mission Training International

Prins, Marina & Willemse, Braam. (2002) *Member Care for Missionaries*. South Africa: Member Care Southern Africa

Punch, Keith F. (2013) *Introduction to Social Research*. 3rd revised edition. Los Angeles/London/New Delhi/Singapore/Washington DC: Sage Publications Ltd.

Rowe, Katie. (2018) *Closer to the truth about current missionary attrition*. Accessed on: 17th April 2018 at: http://www.alifeoverseas.com/closer-to-the-truth-about-current-missionary-attrition-an-initial-analysis-of-results/

Sapsford, Roger. (2006) *Survey Research*. 2nd revised edition. Los Angeles/London/New Delhi/Singapore/Washington DC: SAGE Publications Ltd.

Sarantakos, Sotirios. (1998) *Social Research*. 2nd revised edition. UK/USA: Palgrave Macmillan

Schaefer, Frauke C & Schaefer, Charles A. (2012) *Trauma & Resilience*. Self-published by the authors.

Scovholt, Thomas M. & Trotter-Mathison, Michelle. (2016) *The Resilient Practitioner*. Third Edition. UK: Routledge

Seale, Clive. (1998) *Researching Society & Culture*. Los Angeles/London/New Delhi/Singapore/Washington DC: Sage Publications Ltd

Selvey, David. (2015) *The Truth of Missionary Attrition*. Accessed on 12th June 2018 at: https://blogs.faithlafayette.org/2015/10/24/the-cost-of-missionary-attrition/

Selvey, David, (2015) *Missionary Retention*. Accessed on 9th April 2018 at: https://blogs.faithlafayette.org/missions/missionary-retention/

Shepherd, David. L. (2014) *Promoting Missionary Mutual Care Through Spiritual Community*. Accessed on 7th May 2018 at: http://digitalcommons.georgefox.edu/cgi/viewcontent.cgi?article=1085&context=dmin

Steffen, Tom & McKinney Davis, Lois. (2008) *Encountering Missionary Life and Work*. Grand Rapids Michigan: Baker Academic

Strand, Mark A., Pinkston, Lauren M., Chen, Alice I., Richardson, Jarrett W. (2015) 'Mental Health of Cross-Cultural Healthcare Missionaries', *Journal of Psychology and Theology*, vol. 43, 4: pp.283-293. Accessed on 15th July at: http://web.a.ebscohost.com/ehost/pdfviewer/pdfviewer?vid=3&sid=92a3c5be-89a6-457c-a5fe-ce7c54aa3d0b%40sessionmgr4007

Strange, Dan. (ed.) (2017) 'The Best Possible Gift'. Accessed on 27th August 2018 at: The best possible gift by Oak Hill College - issuu

Takamoto, Susan Plumb. (2003) *Liminality and the North American missionary adjustment process in Japan*. Fuller Theological Seminary, PhD thesis. Received directly from the author.

Taylor, William D., Van Der Meer, Antonia, Reimer Reg. (2012) *Sorrow & Blood: Christian Mission in Contexts of Suffering, Persecution, and Martyrdom (Globalization of Mission)*. Pasadena: William Carey Library.

Taylor, William D. (2002) 'Revisiting a Provocative Theme: The Attrition of Longer-Term Missionaries', *Missiology* 30 Issue 1, Accessed on 13th June 2018 at: http://journals.sagepub.com/doi/pdf/10.1177/009182960203000105

Taylor, William D. (1999) 'Mission Frontiers' Missionary Attrition Series - Part 1: Examining the Faces of Attrition'. Accessed on 13th June 2018 at: http://www.missionfrontiers.org/issue/article/mission-frontiers-missionary-attrition-series-part-1

Taylor, William D. (1997) *Too Valuable to Lose*. Pasadena: William Carey Library

Thomas, Gary. (No date) 'Sacred Pathways - Chi Alpha Discipleship Tool' Accessed on 21st May 2019 at: https://irp-cdn.multiscreensite.com/2988a589/files/uploaded/sacred-pathways.pdf

Thompson, Craig. (2018) 'What is the Average Length of Service for Missionaries on the Field? The Long and the Short of It' Accessed on 29th June 2020 at: https://www.alifeoverseas.com/what-is-the-average-length-of-service-for-missionaries-on-the-field-the-long-and-the-short-of-it/

Thompson, Craig. (2017) *Is Conflict with Teammates Really the Top Reason for Missionaries Leaving the Field?* Accessed on 12th June 2018 at: http://www.alifeoverseas.com/is-conflict-with-teammates-really-the-top-reason-for-missionaries-leaving-the-field/

Trevor, Hugh. (No date) *Japan's Post-War Protestant Churches*. Unpublished – kept by OMF Japan

University of Cambridge. (2018) *Research Integrity - Consent forms and participant information sheets*. Accessed on 6th November 2018 at: https://www.research-integrity.admin.cam.ac.uk/research-ethics/ethics-application-guidance/consent-forms-and-participant-information-sheets

U.S. Department of Labor. (No date) *Family and Medical Leave Act*. Accessed on 26th May 2021 at: Family and Medical Leave (FMLA) | U.S. Department of Labor (dol.gov)

Van Meter, Jim. (2003) *US Report of Findings on Missionary Retention*. Accessed on 14th June 2018 at:
http://www.worldevangelicals.org/resources/rfiles/res3_95_link_1292358708.pdf

Van Ochs, B. (2005) 'Ten Challenges That May Make Staying Home Look Attractive', *Evangelical Missions Quarterly*, Volume 41:2. Accessed on 21st April 2021 at: Ten Challenges That May Make Staying Home Look Attractive - Missio Nexus

Van Ochs, B. (2001) 'Ten Challenges That May Make Going Home Look Attractive', *Evangelical Missions Quarterly*, October-December 2001, Volume 37, Issue 4. Accessed on 9th April 2021 at: Ten Challenges That May Make Going Home Look Attractive - Missio Nexus

Van Pietersom, Tineke., Ehrenreich, John., and Simon, Winnifred. (2006) *Managing Stress in Humanitarian Aid Workers: Guidelines for Good Practice*. Second Edition. Amsterdam: Antares Foundation

Wallace, Ian. (2003) *People in Aid Code of Good Practice in the Management and Support of Aid Personnel*. London: People in Aid
Watts, Duncan. (2017) 'Building Resilience'. Redcliffe College Lecture.

Whittle, Deseree. (1999) 'Missionary Attrition: It's relationship to the spiritual dynamics of the late twentieth century', *Caribbean Journal of Evangelical Theology* (CJET) Accessed on 26/7/2018 at: https://biblicalstudies.org.uk/pdf/cjet/03_68.pdf

Williams, David. (2010) "Pastoral Care of Missionaries: Turning Theory into Practice." *Evangelical Missions Quarterly*. 46(4): 426-432.

Williams, Tim & Ai. (2018) 'Insights into reaching the Japanese', *Resource*, English Teaching & Outreach Forum, 2:19 SIM. Accessed on 24th September 2018 at: https://mailchi.mp/3fbd5ec14983/etof-resource-newsletter?e=21784490e7

Wilson, Michael Todd and Hoffman, Brad. (2007) *Preventing Ministry Failure*. Illinois: IVP

World Evangelical Alliance (Missions Commission). (2010) *ReMAP II: Worldwide Missionary Retention Study & Best Practices*. Accessed on: 2nd August 2018 at: http://www.worldevangelicals.org/resources/rfiles/res3_96_link_1292358945.pdf

Your Enneagram Coach. (2019) *Discover, Explore, and Become Your Best Self*. Accessed on 15th July 2019 at: https://www.yourenneagramcoach.com/

123 Test. (2019). *DISC personality test*. Accessed on 21st May 2019 at: https://www.123test.com/disc-personality-test/

The NIV Bible translation was used where quoted.

About the Author

Janet Dallman was born in the Democratic Republic of Congo, where her parents served as missionaries between 1966 and 1973. Janet lived there until she was five, when her parents decided to leave Congo because of Janet's persistent ill health, the fact that she would have to go to boarding school for her primary education if they stayed, and her mum had trained a Congolese to replace her as a hospital pharmacist.

Janet spent the rest of her childhood in London. Like many missionary kids, she struggled with issues of identity and culture shock, but she came to trust God for herself at the age of nine. Throughout her childhood, Janet felt she would become a missionary somewhere! When she was 21, Janet served for nine months in Senegal with Wycliffe Bible Translators, after which she entered the London School of Theology, where she met her future husband, Peter.

Peter went to seminary feeling called to be a missionary in Japan, whereas Janet had always expected to return to French-speaking Africa. After discovering their mutual liking for one another, they struggled to clarify God's will for them regarding marriage and missionary service. They eventually married in 1994 and went to Japan in 1998 as missionaries with OMF.

Janet and Peter studied Japanese at OMF's Japanese Language and Culture Centre in Sapporo for about two years, before spending a total of four and a half years in church planting in Sapporo. This came to an end due to Peter's struggle with depression, which resulted in Janet and Peter leaving Japan for two and a half years. By God's grace, they returned to Japan and led OMF's Japanese Language and Culture Centre, welcoming new missionaries with OMF for nearly eight years. During that time, Janet's passion for caring for missionaries was fanned into flame and she wrote a devotional book for missionaries titled *Out on a Limb*.

Janet currently serves as Pastoral and Spiritual Care Coordinator for OMF Japan. This pastoral role awakened Janet's desire for further training, leading to her doing a Master's degree in missionary member care at Redcliffe College in the UK, which she completed in 2019.

Printed in Great Britain
by Amazon